NEEDLEPOINT BARGELLO

NEEDLEPOINT BARGELLO

Dorothy Kaestner

Photos by
George F. Kaestner

CHARLES SCRIBNER'S SONS

NEW YORK

Library of Congress Cataloging in Publication Data

Kaestner, Dorothy
    Needlepoint bargello.

    Bibliography: p.
    1. Canvas embroidery—Patterns.   I. Title.
TT778.C3K34   746.4'4   73-14400
ISBN 0-684-16941-X

1 3 5 7 9 11 13 15 17 19 V/P 20 18 16 14 12 10 8 6 4 2

Printed in the United States of America

Design by Pat Smythe

To George who was an important half of this endeavor

ACKNOWLEDGMENTS

My thanks to Mrs. Samuel Pierson, Mrs. Robert McKay and Mrs. Donald Page for allowing me to illustrate their work. Thanks also to Mrs. H. Weller Keever of New Canaan for stitching the Fox tray and to Joan deSelding and Lois Mackey, who work in my shop, for helping me finish some of the pieces. A special thank you goes to my editor, Elinor Parker, for her quiet encouragement; also to Janet Hornberger and Pat Smythe for their cooperation in putting this in order.

Contents

Introduction

After finishing my first book, *Four Way Bargello*, design ideas were still coming to me—so my pencil and needle have been busy ever since. I have compiled 67 more designs for this book. There are 25 four way bargello, 32 regular bargello, 9 needlepoint, and 1 combination.

There are designs inspired by photographs of snowflakes, some oriental-type patterns, fleur-de-lis, and a few projects with finishing instructions.

At times my well of ideas would dry up and then I would see something in a book or magazine that would start a new way of thinking or another color combination. The orange-purple-red Aztec type pattern came to me when I saw a room in these colors pictured in *House Beautiful* a couple of years ago. There were chairs in purple, some in orange and red. There was a printed or embroidered pillow in one of them in an Aztec type design which started me on this piece. As I worked on it, I thought it would be good-looking done in black, brown and white. Then I thought that this coloring would look even better with a more angular pattern. This should make a nice upholstery.

The Oriental designs started with trying to duplicate some of the cloud patterns in bargello and also a border. Then I saw a lovely antique Chinese rug in the book *Color Treasury of Rugs and Tapestries*, published by Crescent Books.

Another group of designs developed from the Dover publication, *Snowcrystals*. A friend brought the book to me thinking I could use it for my four way bargello ideas. But four way bargello has 4 or 8 sides and nearly all snowflakes are 6 sided. I decided to work the patterns in tent stitch. It was a difficult decision as to which ones I would use. One could do a whole book of designs just on snowflakes. I did do five of them.

1

There are also some "mini" four way bargello patterns for coasters or pincushions, a couple of tissue box covers and a wastebasket with finishing instructions, and a tray.

George and I have been giving workshops throughout the country in four way bargello. Through these workshops, I realize many people do not understand charts or charting. It has been a joy to me to teach them how to understand and to make one's own chart for bargello. It has also been a great pleasure to meet all these wonderful people who want to know a little more about bargello and four way bargello. It's so exciting to me to hear them say "I've got it!" and to know someone else is sharing my pleasure.

I must tell a little story on George. He had not done any bargello, let alone four way bargello. On our way to Texas to teach a series of workshops, I taught him how to do both so that he could help me with the workshops. He stumbled a little through the first couple of them but soon became a pro. Now he helps teach quite a bit, and being ambidextrous, he's great with the lefties.

General Working Instructions

DIAGONAL TENT STITCH or BASKET WEAVE STITCH

To work with the grain of the canvas, first place a stitch in the upper right corner of your canvas (assuming that you are working a square). Now examine the weave of the canvas. If the canvas threads which are to be covered next are vertical, (shaded in top diagram), then your next stitch will be placed to the left of the corner stitch. If, on the other hand, the next row of stitching shows horizontal threads (shaded in second diagram), then your next stitch will be below the corner stitch. In other words, you work from the top down when covering vertical canvas threads or from the bottom up when covering the horizontal canvas threads. The third diagram shows the progression of rows.

I have found that this method keeps your stitches more even. When worked in the opposite direction, one row looks a little different than the other. Try working a small area as described, then work a small area in the opposite manner and you will see the difference.

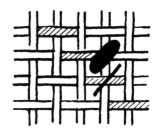

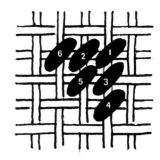

BARGELLO

This is a straight up and down stitch covering two or more threads of the canvas. The basic bargello is a stitch covering four threads and stepping up or down by two threads. This is referred to as a 4-2 step.

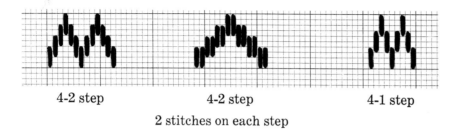

4-2 step   4-2 step   4-1 step

2 stitches on each step

PLEASE NOTE: In most of my charts for bargello and four way bargello, each *square* of the chart refers to a *thread* of the canvas, so if there are *four squares* filled on the chart for a stitch, you will cover *four threads* on the canvas.

Whenever you start bargello, decide which part of the pattern is going to be the center, then start with that at the center of the canvas. From the center, work to the left, then go back to the center and work that row to the right. Now you can work the remaining rows all the way across.

FOUR WAY BARGELLO

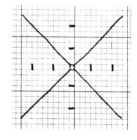

Find the center of the canvas and with pencil outline the center hole. Then draw diagonal lines as shown in diagram. DO NOT USE A RULER. These lines must be accurate or you will be wondering why your pattern does not come out right at the mitre lines. NOTE: If you are going to use a light color tent stitch background, do not use pencil to mark the mitre lines. Use a colored piece of sewing thread and stitch the lines in as shown in photo. When you finish the bargello design, all you need do is to pull out the sewing thread and there are no pencil lines to show through. The pencil lines do not show through when the entire piece is worked in bargello.

When working from the charts, be sure to count the center square as 1 in each of the 4 directions. Otherwise you may read the center stitches as covering only 3 threads instead of 4 threads.

CANVAS

Canvas is supposed to be an even weave material. It is not always so. Also, the count of the mesh varies from roll to roll, as you will see by some of the measurements of patterns I list. In listing measurements of the four way bargello pieces, I wrote they SHOULD measure, etc.

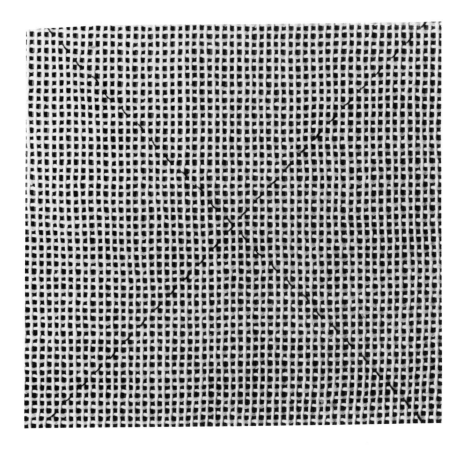

Sometimes we get a roll of #10 canvas and it might count to be 9 or 11. This makes a difference in the finished size of the pattern. #13 and #14 canvases have come through at 13½. Your store owner cannot help this. He has to take what the looms have produced. So you must decide whether you want to have the design slightly larger or smaller.

I have found that some people were using a larger mesh canvas to do some of the designs from my *Four Way Bargello* book than the mesh I mentioned. They did not count off the number of threads of canvas used to make the design to find out how large a piece of canvas was needed. Many times this left them with too small a piece to fit the entire pattern on. That is why, in this book, I have given approximate measurements when I felt it necessary. This will make it much easier and quicker for you or your shop owner to determine the size piece of canvas needed.

It is almost impossible to buy a roll of canvas today without knots or flaws. If one tried to cut canvas to avoid flaws there would be considerable waste.

It is very easy to repair a knotted canvas or one which you may have accidently cut when snipping out stitches. Cut the knot out, then take a piece of the thread out of the canvas at the edge. Put this thread through your needle and weave it in, copying the weave of the cut thread. The beginning and end of this new thread should overlap the cut part by an inch in each direction. When you start stitching, just work over the double threads as if they were one.

If you have other canvas which has a finer thread in the weave, you can use this. Then the double thread will be easier to work over.

CANVAS—YARN CHART

Persian Yarn (3 2 ply strands)

Mesh size	Bargello	Tent Stitch
10	4 or 5 strands	3 strands
12	3 strands	2 or 3 strands
13 & 14	3 strands	2 strands
16	2 strands	1 strand (this is thin)
18	2 strands	1 strand

Nantucket Needleworks' Yarn (4 2 ply strands)

12	6 strands	all 4 strands
13 & 14	5 strands	4 strands
16	4 strands	3 strands
18	3 strands	2 strands

Elsa Williams' Yarn (4 single ply strands)

12	6 ply (Cut a length twice as long. Pull a ply out, then fold in half in the needle.)	4 ply (as is)
13 & 14	as is	as is
16	as is	3 ply
18	3 ply	2 ply

The persian yarn color numbers refer to Paternayan yarns.

Scrolls and Frets 1

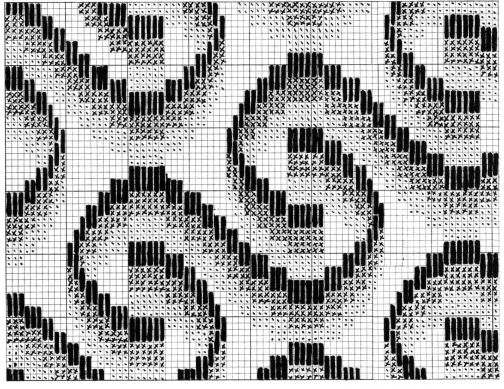

See Color Plate 1 *page 9*

Coral scrolls on beige

This is a 4-2 step regular bargello worked on #14
mono canvas with 3 strands of persian yarn.
The colors used were:

▌	210 red
✗	843 coral red
╲	853 coral red
▯	020 beige background

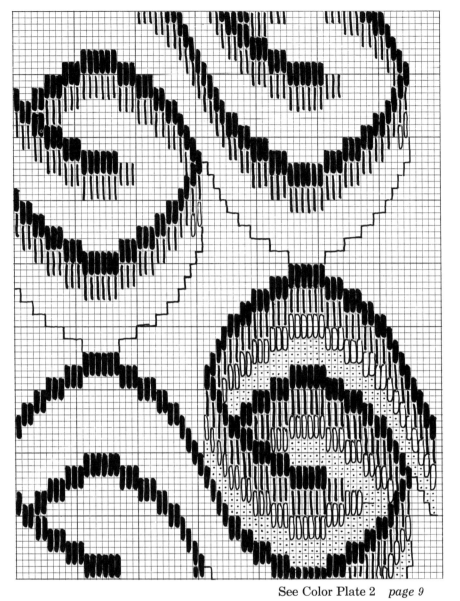

See Color Plate 2 *page 9*

Gold larger scrolls on orange

This is also a 4-2 step regular bargello worked on
#14 mono canvas with 3 strands of persian yarn.
The colors used were:

511 dark gold

433 gold

445 gold

455 gold

965 orange background

Plate 1

Coral scrolls on beige

Chart, page 7

Plate 2

Gold larger scrolls on orange

Chart, page 8

Plate 3
Gold and aqua fret
Chart, page 17

Plate 4
Green and turquoise fret
Chart, page 18

Plate 5

Green spheres on pink

Chart, page 19

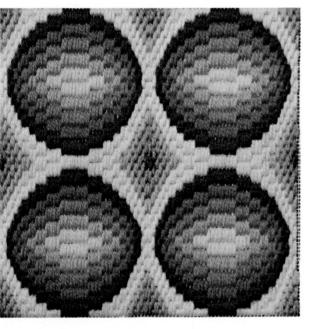

Plate 6

Violet blue and turquoise spheres on poles

Chart, page 20

Plate 7

Rust to coral spheres and green diamonds

Chart, page 21

Plate 8   Red and black overlapping squares   *Chart pages 22-23*

Plate 9

Red white and blue

Chart, page 25

Plate 10

Turquoise, purple and green

Chart, page 27

13

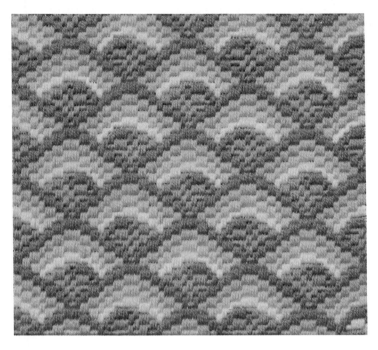

Plate 11

Pink, blue and white clouds

Chart, page 28

Plate 12

Blue clouds on off-white

Chart, page 29

Plate 13

Green clouds reversed and joined

Chart, page 30

Plate 14
Cresting waves
Chart, page 31

Plate 15
Mrs. Donald Page's chair
Chart, page 41

Plate 16

Coral T border with white clouds on aqua

Chart, page 32

Plate 17

Gold swastika border pillow

Charts, pages 42-43

Gold and aqua fret

A 4-2 step regular bargello was used for this design and for the green and turquoise fret as well. Both were worked on #14 mono canvas with 3 strands of persian yarn.
The colors used were:

▌ 433 gold

　793 aqua background

See Color Plate 3 *page 10*

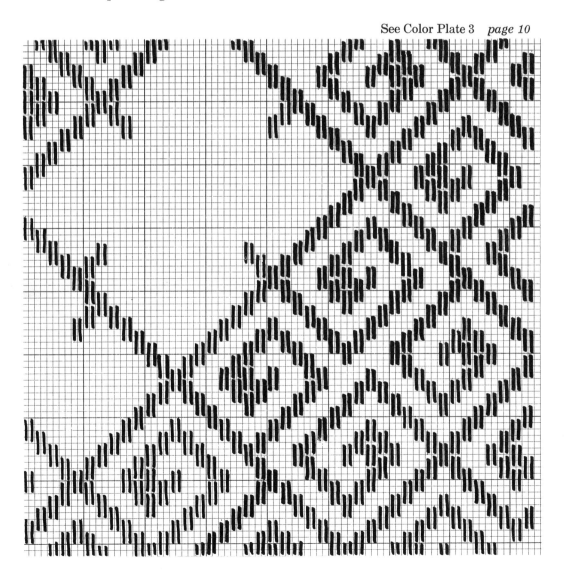

See Color Plate 4 *page 10*

Green and turquoise fret

The colors used were:

559 dark green

G64 green

738 turquoise background

Spheres and Squares 2

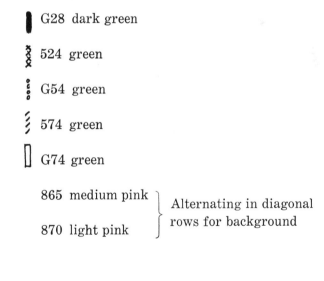

All of the sphere designs are a 4-2 step regular bargello.

Green spheres on pink

A #14 mono canvas was used with 3 strands of persian yarn.

The colors used were:

G28 dark green

524 green

G54 green

574 green

G74 green

865 medium pink ⎱ Alternating in diagonal
870 light pink   ⎰ rows for background

See Color Plate 5

page 11

See Color Plate 6   *page 11*

Violet blue and turquoise spheres on poles

This was also on #14 mono canvas using 3 strands
of persian yarn for the bargello and 2 strands for
the background which was worked in tent stitch.
The colors used were:

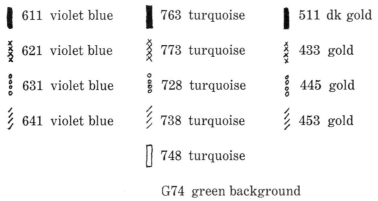

▌ 611 violet blue	▐ 763 turquoise	▌ 511 dk gold
✗✗✗ 621 violet blue	⟩⟩⟩ 773 turquoise	✗✗✗ 433 gold
⦿ 631 violet blue	⦿ 728 turquoise	⦿ 445 gold
⁄⁄⁄ 641 violet blue	⁄⁄⁄ 738 turquoise	⁄⁄⁄ 453 gold
	⧠ 748 turquoise	

G74 green background

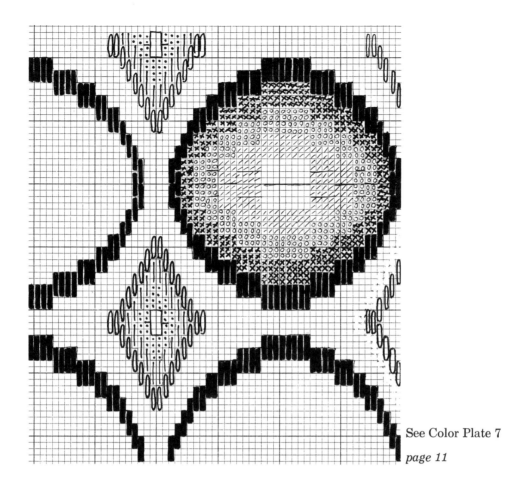

See Color Plate 7

page 11

Rust to coral spheres and green diamonds

#12 mono canvas and 3 strands of persian yarn.
The colors used were:

- 225 rust
- 273 rust
- 278 rust
- 853 coral
- 870 coral
- 559 green
- G64 green
- 574 green
- G74 green

014 beige background

21

Squares

All of the square patterns are a 4-2 step worked on #16 mono canvas.

Red and black overlapping squares

I used Nantucket Needleworks yarn for this regular bargello piece, which measures 12″ across. The colors used were:

25 red

120 black

1 white

109 grey background

See Color Plate 8

22

page 12

23

Red white and blue

This is a four way bargello worked with
Elsa Williams yarn in the following colors:

▌ N521 blue

▏ N113 red

▐ N900 white

This piece measures approx. 11″ square

See Color Plate 9

25

Turquoise, purple and green

This is another four way bargello using Nantucket Needleworks yarn. My piece measures 13″.
The colors used were:

- 62 light turquoise
- 66 turquoise
- 63 turquoise
- 64 turquoise
- 65 turquoise
- 45 light purple
- 46 purple
- 47 purple
- 44 red purple
- 76 light green
- 77 green
- 78 green
- 79 green

See Color Plate 10

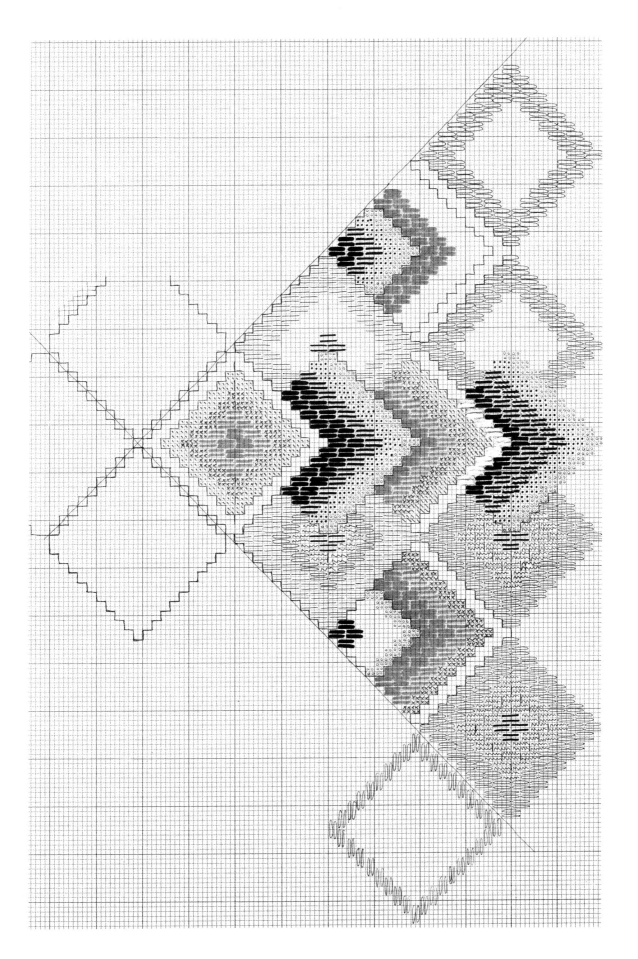

3 Oriental Type Patterns

Pink, blue and white clouds

This is a small allover pattern in regular bargello.
4-2 step. I used #13 mono canvas with all 3
strands of persian yarn.
The colors used were:

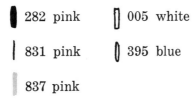

282 pink   005 white

831 pink   395 blue

837 pink

See Color Plate 11 *page 14*

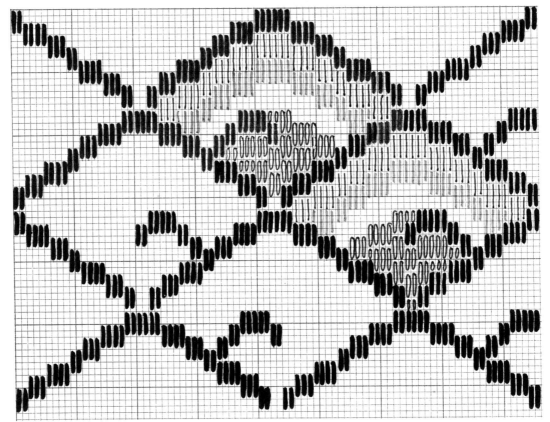

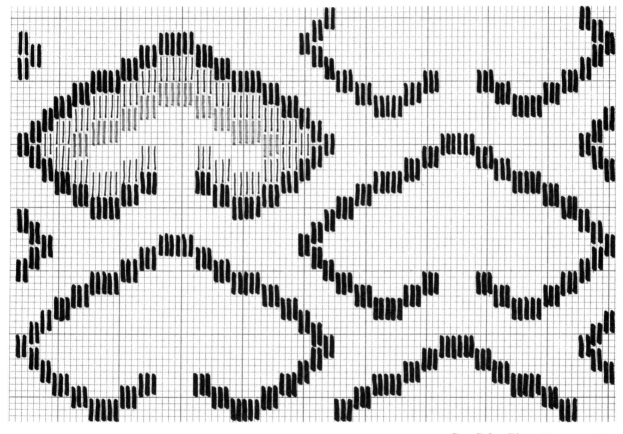

See Color Plate 12   *page 14*

Blue clouds on off-white

This is another all over regular bargello, 4-2 step.
However, this time the clouds are separated with
2 rows of background. #14 mono canvas was used
with 3 strands of persian yarn.
The colors used were:

330 blue

385 blue

756 blue

011 off-white background

29

See Color Plate 13   *page 14*

Green clouds reversed and joined

When every other cloud is turned upside down
and joined they create little patterns between
them. #14 mono canvas was used with 3 strands
of persian yarn. This is a 4-2 step.
The colors used were:

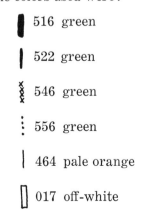

516 green

522 green

546 green

556 green

464 pale orange

017 off-white

30

Cresting waves

Here is another regular bargello—4-2 step. Ten
shades have been used in order to get the depth
of the trough to the foam of the crest. If you
turn the design sideways, there is an illusion
of sea horses. #13 mono canvas was used with
3 strands of persian yarn.

The colors used were:

▌	365 blue	▎	756 aqua
▎	334 blue	⚡	763 turquoise
✕	330 blue	⦚	340 green
⦙	385 blue	⋮	758 aqua
⫽	395 blue	▯	005 white

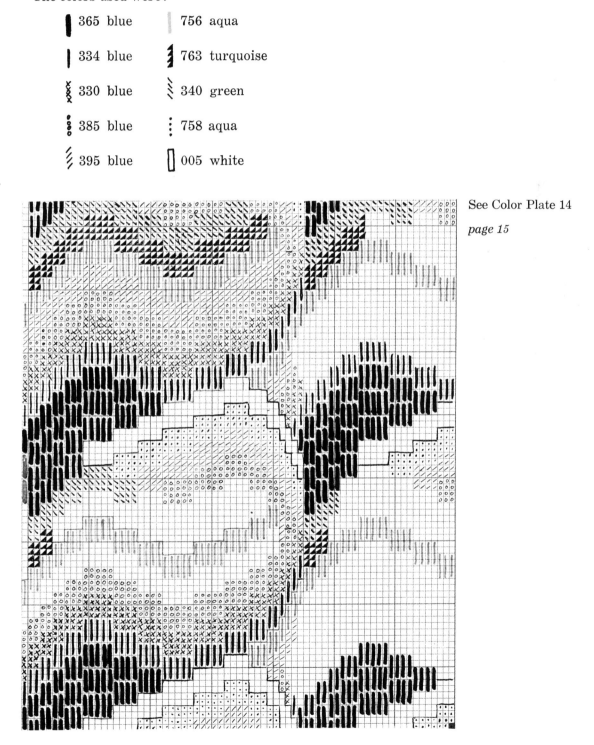

See Color Plate 14

page 15

See Color Plate 16   *page 16*

Coral T border with white clouds on aqua

The T border is done in a form of four way
bargello and the clouds in regular bargello—
the background is in tent stitch. #14 mono canvas
was used with 3 strands of persian yarn for the
bargello and 2 strands for the tent stitch.
NOTE: The chart for the border and clouds is
different than my usual method of charting. The
LINES of the chart refer to the threads of the
canvas. Also, in order to get good corners, I used
stitches over one thread, which I seldom do in
four way bargello.
The colors used were 843 for the border, 005 for
the clouds and 765 for the background.

Plate 18

Yellow and turquoise

Chart, page 45

Plate 19

Yellow and orange

Chart, page 45

33

Plate 20

Blue, green and yellow green

Chart, page 48

Plate 21

Green leaf border

Chart, page 46

Plate 22

Orange woven cables

Chart, page 49

Plate 23

Blue cable strip

Chart, page 48

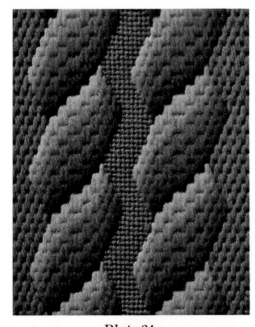

Plate 24

Gold separated cables on blue

Chart, page 50

Plate 25

Red separated cables with pink and white

Chart, page 50

Plate 26

Gold fleur-de-lis on turquoise

Chart, page 52

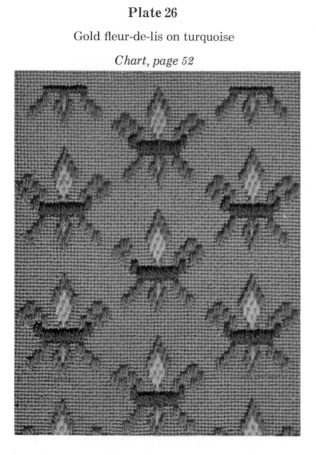

Plate 27

Pink fleur-de-lis with green bands

Chart, page 53

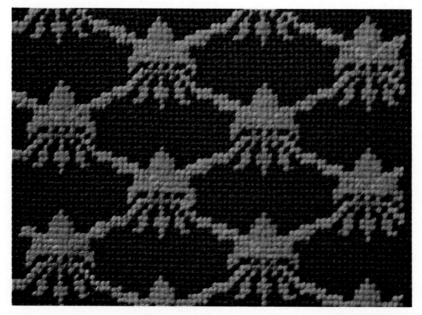

Plate 28

Yellow fleur-de-lis on royal blue

Chart, page 51

36

Plate 29 Gold and blue four way bargello *Chart, page 54*

Plate 30

Black, grey and white

Chart, page 56

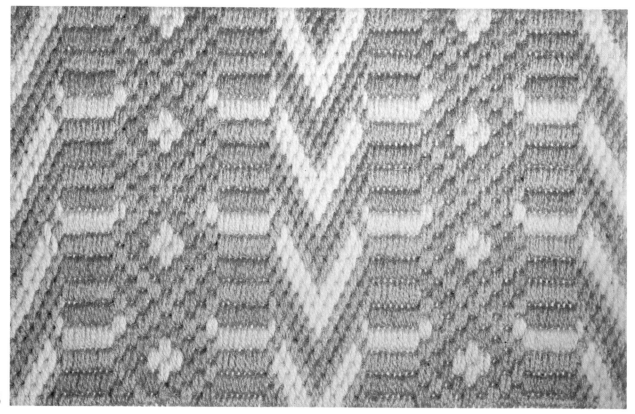

Plate 31   Copper and burnt orange   *Chart, page 67*

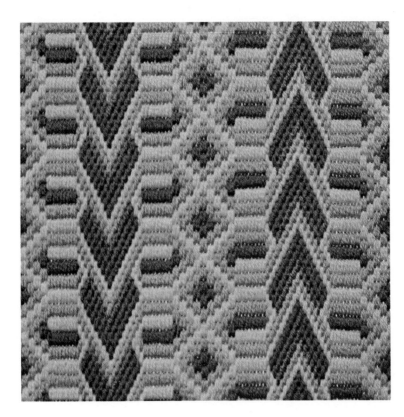

Plate 32

Greens with blue

Chart, page 65

Plate 33

Blues with light green

Chart, page 65

39

Plate 34

Shocking pink and gold

Chart, page 66

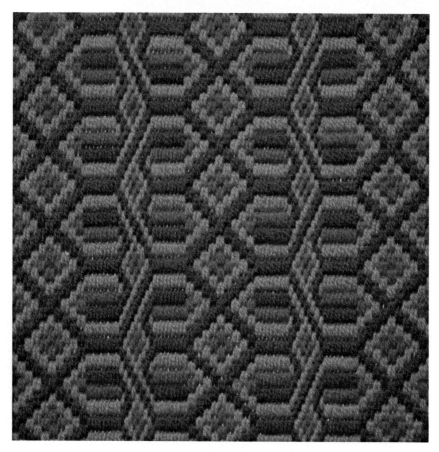

Plate 35

Purple and pink

Chart, page 66

Mrs. Donald Page's chair

Mrs. Page was in one of my classes at Silvermine Guild when I was working with some of the cloud patterns. She is very fond of Chinese design so asked me to work out a cloud pattern for this chair. I think the clouds follow the contour quite well. She used #14 mono canvas, 4-2 step bargello and a tent stitch background.

The colors used were:

540 green

594 dull green

755 turquoise

760 turquoise

765 turquoise

565 yellow green background

See Color Plate 15 *page 15*

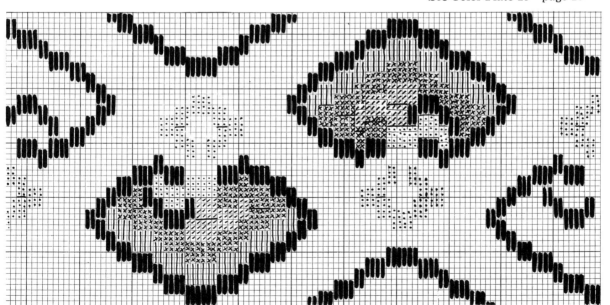

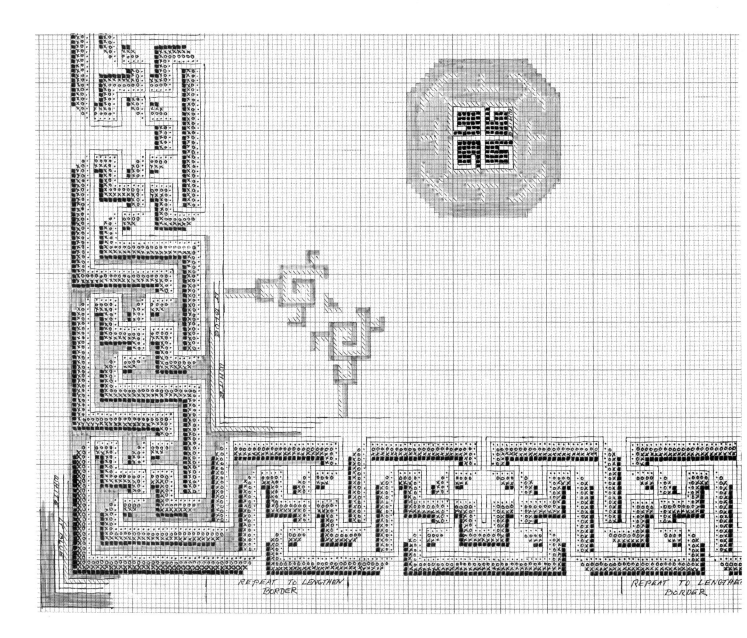

Gold swastika border pillow

This is a typical Chinese border. A photo of an antique Chinese rug in *Color Treasury of Rugs and Tapestries* inspired me to work this in needlepoint using the colors shown in the book. I did not try to use all the motifs which were in the center of the rug, but chose only two to keep it simpler. The border can be extended by adding more repeats of the sections marked. The background is worked with one strand each of 447 and 457 gold. I used #14 mono canvas with 2 strands of persian yarn.

This pattern as is measures 15″ on 14 mesh canvas, 16″ on 12 mesh canvas, 19¼″ on 10 mesh canvas

The colors used were:

42

- ▪ 427 gold
- ✕ 447 gold
- ○ 457 gold
- · 467 gold
- ▫ 438 light yellow
- ╱ 322 medium blue
-    781 light blue
-    005 white
- ▪ 108 charcoal

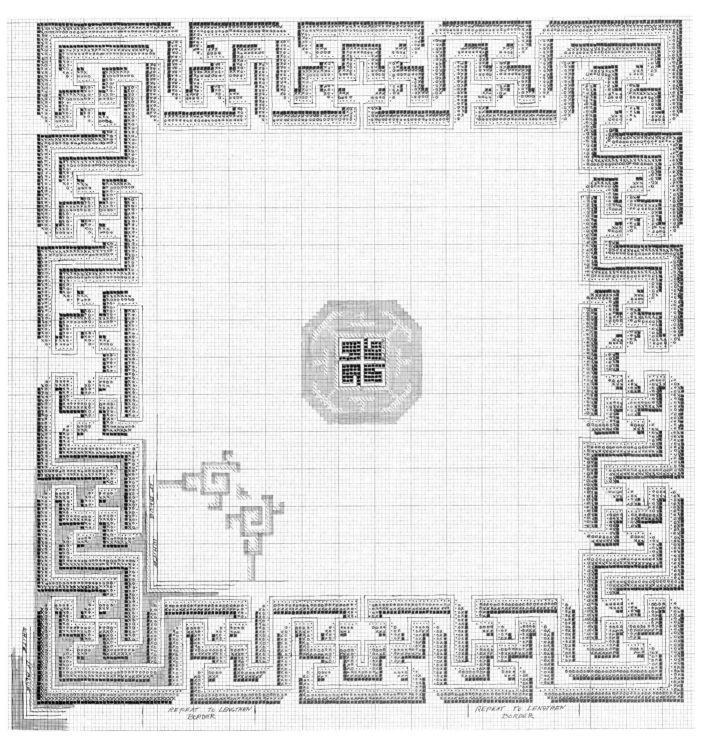

REPEAT TO LENGTHEN
BORDER

REPEAT TO LENGTHEN
BORDER

See Color Plate 17   *page 16*

 Cables

All of the cable patterns are a 4-2 step bargello.
The border on this page was not stitched. I made
the chart so as to show how to turn the cable
around a corner.

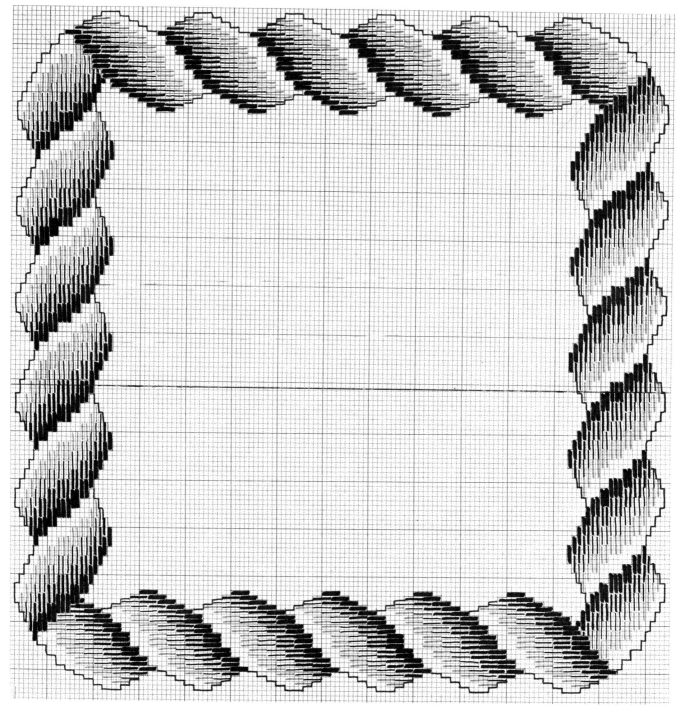

44

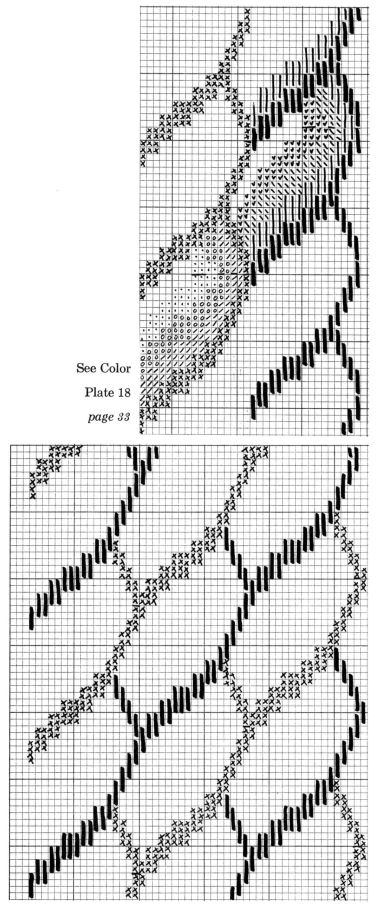

See Color
Plate 18

page 33

Yellow and turquoise

In this pattern the cables are fitted together. I used #14 mono canvas with 3 strands of persian yarn.
The colors used were:

550	yellow green	750	dark turquoise
Y52	yellow	755	turquoise
Y56	yellow	760	turquoise
Y58	yellow	765	turquoise
Y68	yellow	032	pale blue

Yellow and orange

The cable is the same as no. 2 but the colors are carried off on the diagonal instead of vertical. #14 mono canvas was used with 3 strands persian yarn.
The colors used were:

550	yellow green
Y52	yellow
Y56	yellow
Y58	yellow
Y68	yellow
958	dark red orange
960	orange
965	orange
975	orange
457	orange yellow

See Color Plate 19   *page 33*

45

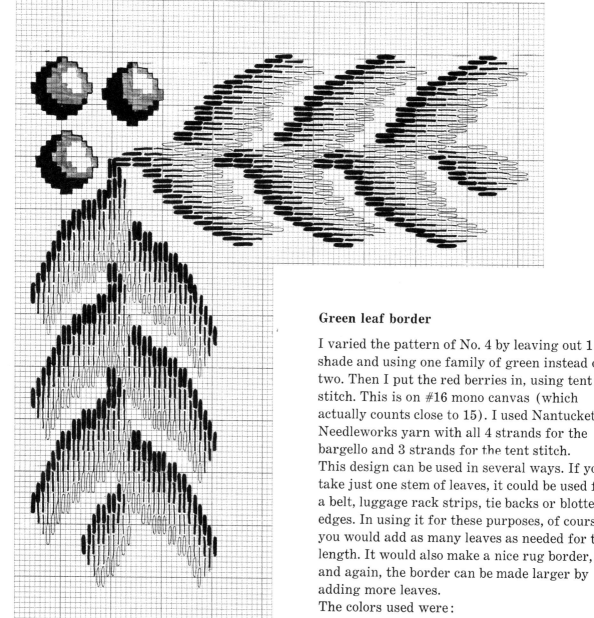

See Color Plate 21

page 34

Green leaf border

I varied the pattern of No. 4 by leaving out 1 shade and using one family of green instead of two. Then I put the red berries in, using tent stitch. This is on #16 mono canvas (which actually counts close to 15). I used Nantucket Needleworks yarn with all 4 strands for the bargello and 3 strands for the tent stitch.

This design can be used in several ways. If you take just one stem of leaves, it could be used for a belt, luggage rack strips, tie backs or blotter edges. In using it for these purposes, of course you would add as many leaves as needed for the length. It would also make a nice rug border, and again, the border can be made larger by adding more leaves.

The colors used were:

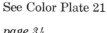 79 dark green

79 green

77 green

76 green

34 dark red

28 red

27 pink

1 white background

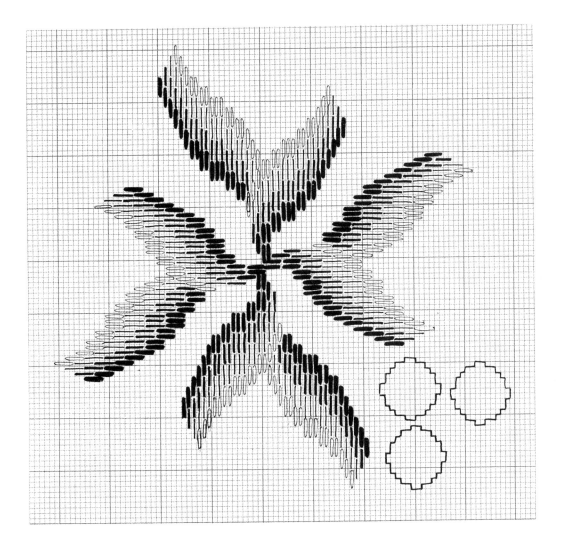

On #16 canvas a complete square border measures
approx. 12½″
On my "#16" canvas it measures about 13½″.
On #14 canvas it should measure about 14⅓″
On #12 canvas it should measure about 16½″
On #10 canvas it should measure about 20″

If the two outside corners were joined, the four
stems of leaves would radiate out from the center.
Then the berries could be placed in each of the
four corners as shown in the chart. This chart
shows how to place the stems at the center.
The center square of the chart is counted for the
upper stitch (over 4 threads) and is counted
again for the lower stitch. (It is also over
4 threads.)

47

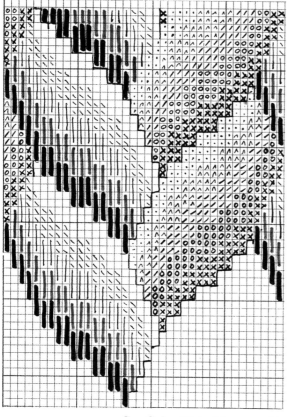

See Color Plate 20   *page 34*

Blue green and yellow green

This is the same cable except that every other one is reversed. It was worked on #14 mono canvas with 3 strands of persian yarn. The colors used were:

504 dark blue green

G28 blue green

G30 blue green

G32 blue green

G38 blue green

G54 dark yellow green

G64 yellow green

574 yellow green

G74 yellow green

48   575 yellow green

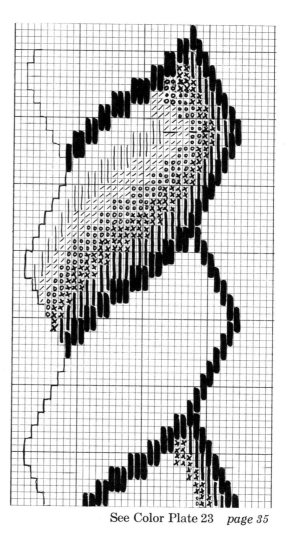

See Color Plate 23   *page 35*

Blue cable strip

This is a larger cable pattern which would make a good belt or luggage rack strip. I used #14 mono canvas with 3 strands of persian yarn for the bargello and 2 strands for the tent stitch. The colors used were:

310 bright navy

740 dark blue

742 blue

752 blue

754 blue

756 blue

758 blue

Y52 yellow background

Orange woven cables

This is another larger variation making a woven pattern. Even though I used 3 shades of lavender between the cables, I think one color there would make the cables more pronounced. This was worked on #14 mono canvas with 3 strands of persian yarn.

The colors used were:

958 dark red orange

960 orange

965 orange

975 orange

457 orange yellow

467 orange yellow

615 dark lavender

618 lavender

620 lavender

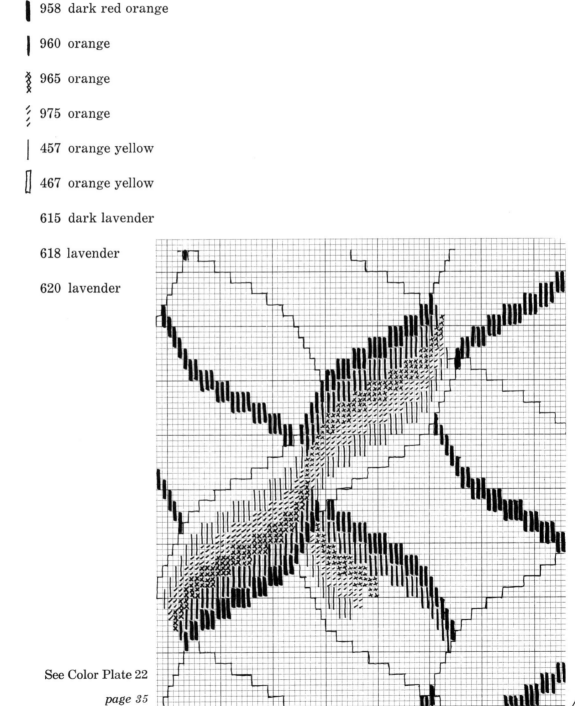

See Color Plate 22

page 35

49

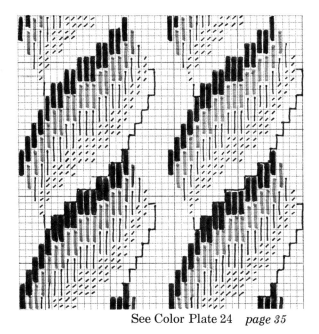

Gold separated cables on blue

This double cable shows some of the blue background worked in bargello and some in tent stitch. As shown, it would make a good luggage rack strip or it may fit some blotter ends. One cable only would make a good belt or guitar strap. It was worked on #16 canvas with Elsa Williams' yarn in the following colors:

▌	N301 dark gold	⁝	N304 gold
▐	N302 gold	▯	N305 gold
▍	N303 gold		N504 blue background

See Color Plate 24 *page 35*

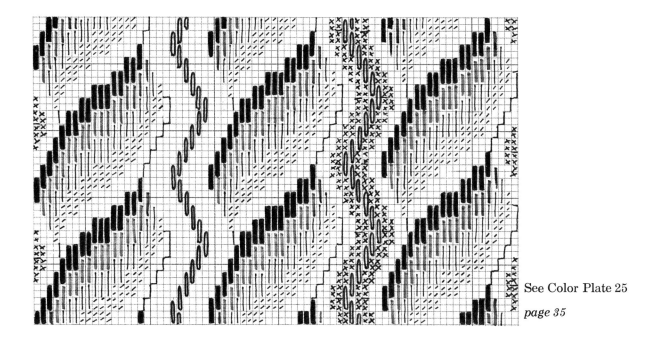

See Color Plate 25

page 35

Red separated cables with pink and white

This is the same cable separated a little more and each cable row moved up by ½ a stitch from the one to its left. It makes a little wider band when using just the two cables, but could be continued as an all over pattern as the chart suggests. It was worked on #16 canvas with Elsa Williams' yarn in the following colors:

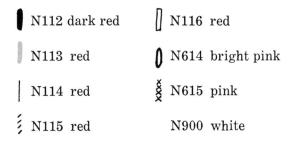

▌	N112 dark red	▯	N116 red
▐	N113 red	◖	N614 bright pink
▍	N114 red	⨯	N615 pink
⁝	N115 red		N900 white

50

Fleur-de-Lis 5

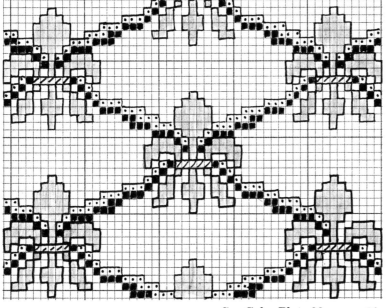

See Color Plate 28 *page 36*

Yellow fleur-de-lis on royal blue

This is a small tent stitch design worked on #16
mono canvas with 3 strands of Nantucket
Needleworks yarn.
The colors used were:

■ 53 blue

╱ 8 gold

• 1 white

▨ 7 bright yellow

61 royal blue background

See Color Plate 26   *page 36*

Gold fleur-de-lis on turquoise

This is a 4-2 step regular bargello. I used #14
mono canvas with 3 strands of persian yarn for
the bargello and 2 strands for the tent stitch.
The colors used were:

▌ 433 dark gold

❨ 445 gold

❘ 455 gold

    760 turquoise background

See Color Plate 27 *page 36*

Pink fleur-de-lis with green bands

In this piece there are two different sizes of
fleur-de-lis. It was worked on #12 mono canvas
using 3 strands of persian yarn for the 4-2 step
bargello and 2 strands for the tent stitch.
The color used were:

821 dark pink

827 pink

828 pink

G74 green

592 light green background

See Color Plate 29   *page 37*

Gold and blue four way bargello

This is practically the same pattern as No. 3 but worked as a four way bargello. I added another row to the bands and a small pattern in the center. The center design could be used alone as a coaster or pincushion. This piece was worked on #16 mono canvas with all 4 strands of Nantucket Needleworks yarn for bargello and 3 strands for tent stitch.

The colors used were:

| 60 dark blue

| 59 medium blue

ⵝ 11 dark gold

◖ 10 gold

‖ 13 yellow

3 pale yellow background

By actual measurement this "#16" canvas is closer to a 15 count. The design measures 12½".
On a 14 mesh it would measure about 13¼"
On a 13 mesh it would measure about 14¼"
On a 12 mesh it would measure about 15⅓"
On a 10 mesh it would measure about 18½"

6 Variations on a Theme

In this group of designs, I started with the black, grey and white. Then I proceeded to move the pattern around as in those following. They are all regular bargello and a 4-2 step using 3 strands of persian yarn.

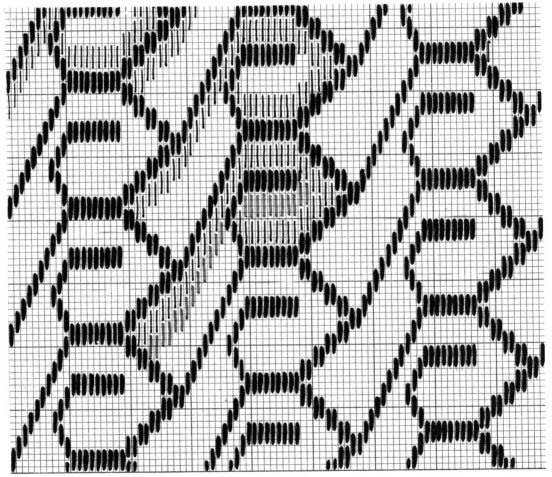

See Color Plate 30   *page 38*

Black, grey and white

This was worked on #14 mono canvas. Each vertical row of the design is higher than the one on its left.
The colors used were:

❙ 050 black		▌ 186 grey	
❘ 182 grey		〛 005 white	

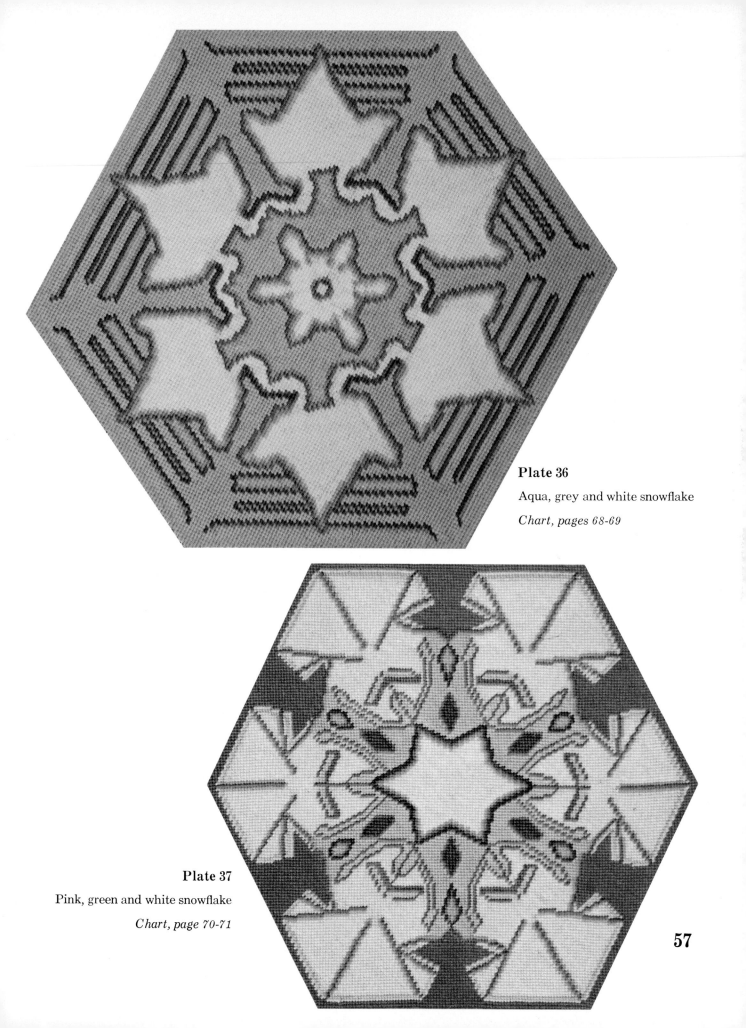

Plate 36

Aqua, grey and white snowflake

Chart, pages 68-69

Plate 37

Pink, green and white snowflake

Chart, page 70-71

Plate 38

Yellow, black and white snowflake

Chart, pages 76-77

Plate 39

Purple, black and brown snowflake

Chart, pages 74-75

58

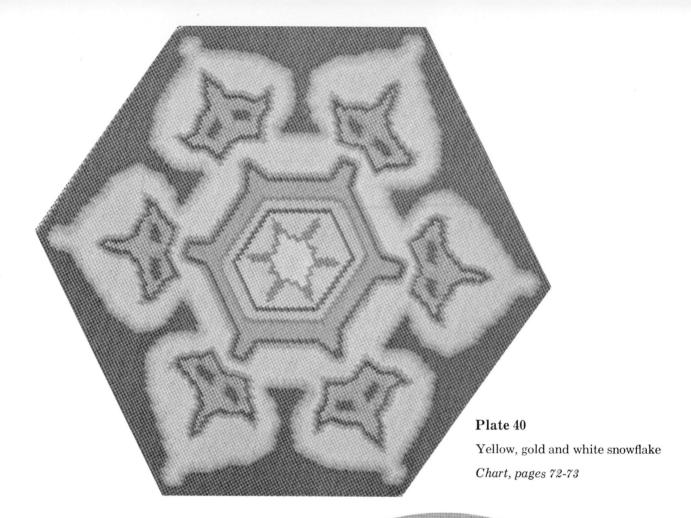

Plate 40

Yellow, gold and white snowflake

Chart, pages 72-73

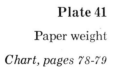

Plate 41

Paper weight

Chart, pages 78-79

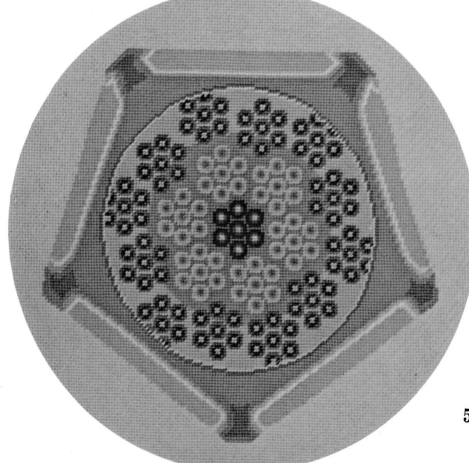

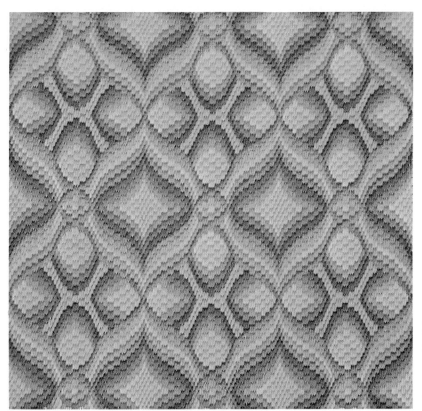

Plate 42

Turquoise and green
regular bargello
Chart, page 81

Plate 44

Copper and grey four way bargello
Chart, page 85

Plate 43

Strawberry Patch four way bargello

Chart, page 82

Plate 45

Red and white

Chart, page 87

Plate 46

Blue, aqua, lavender center
square and border

Chart, pages 88-89

61

Plate 47

Rose and blue with contour border

Chart, pages 90-91

Plate 48

Copper and grey

Chart, pages 94-95

Plate 49

Gold outline with pinks

Chart, pages 92-93

Plate 50   Blue, aqua, green and orange hanging   *Chart, pages 96-97*

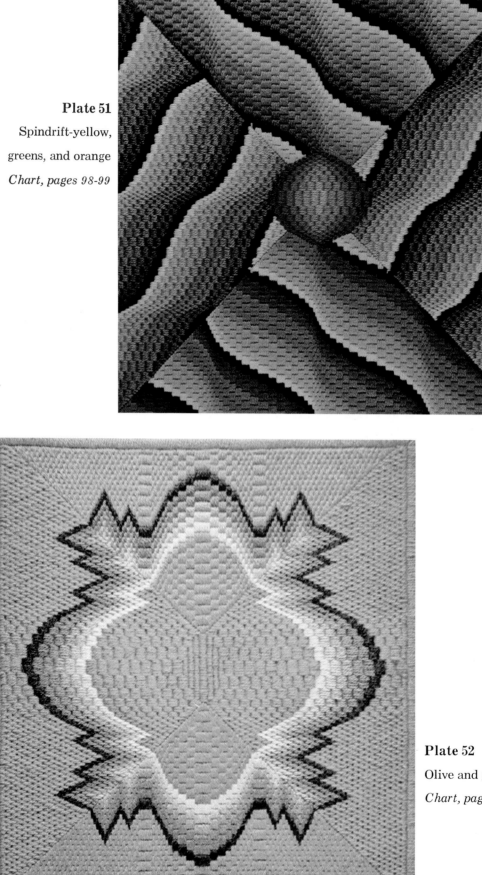

Plate 51

Spindrift-yellow,

greens, and orange

Chart, pages 98-99

Plate 52

Olive and green oblong border

Chart, page 101

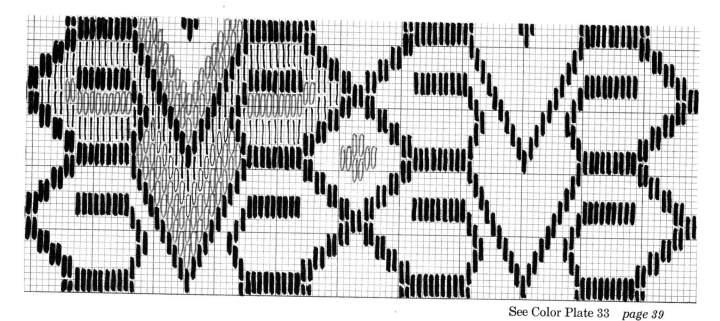

See Color Plate 33   *page 39*

Blues with light green (above)

By turning every other pointed part of the design
in the opposite direction and on the same level,
I got diamonds and overlapping diamond points.
#14 mono canvas.
The colors used were:

611 dark blue

621 medium blue

631 light blue

G74 green

Greens with blue (below)

One half of this pattern is the same as No. 2,
but the other half is turned upside down.
#14 mono canvas.
The colors used were:

611 blue

G74 light green

G64 green

G54 green

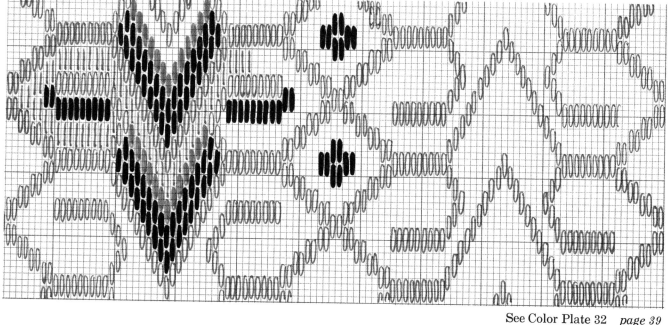

See Color Plate 32   *page 39*

See Color Plate 34 *page 40*

See Color Plate 35 *page 40*

Shocking pink and gold (top left)

This time, I turned every other motif upside down which made the diamond points become complete diamonds. #14 mono canvas.

The colors used were:

| 827 dark pink

| 659 light pink

| 433 dark gold

| 445 light gold

Copper and burnt orange

When making the chart for No. 2, I made a mistake in the number of stitches in the diamond points, so I decided to use this as another pattern. This is on #12 mono canvas.
The colors used were:

| 419 medium copper

| 425 light copper

| 424 burnt orange

| 444 light burnt orange

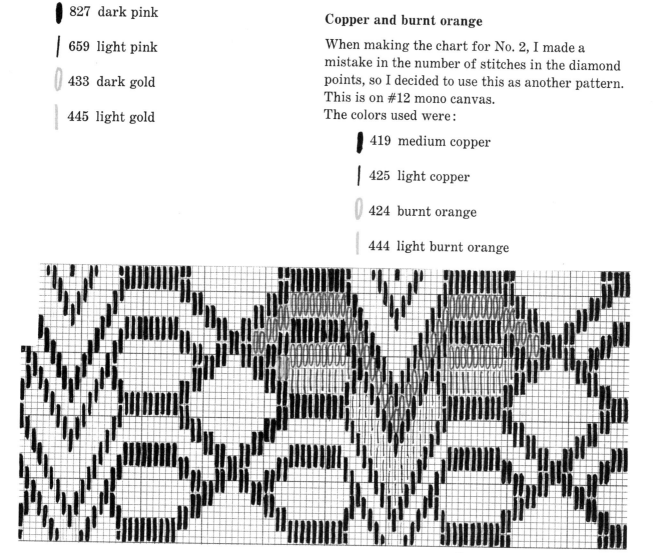

See Color Plate 31   *page 38*

Purple and pink (bottom left)

I used the same pattern as No. 4 but moved one vertical row of motifs so that it fits where the large diamonds are in No. 4. #14 mono canvas.
The colors used were:

| 633 dark purple

| 653 light purple

| 855 pink

67

7 Five Snowflakes and a Paperweight

All of these pieces were worked on #12 canvas in tent stitch using all 4 strands of Nantucket Needleworks yarn.

Aqua, grey and white snowflake

The colors are:

    1 White

  ✕ 64 aqua

  • 62 light aqua

  ╱ 63 aqua

  ■ 65 aqua

      109 grey

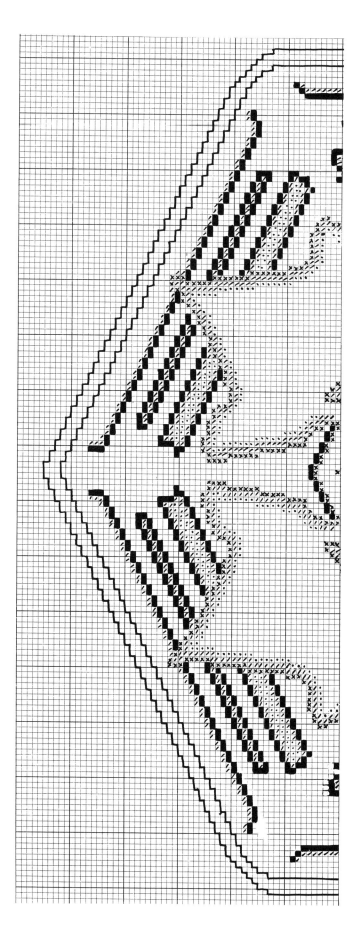

1 white

109 grey

Pink, green and white snowflake

The colors are:

   1 white

• 29 light pink

∕ 76 light green

✕ 77 medium green

■ 78 dark green

▨ 109 grey

   30 bright pink

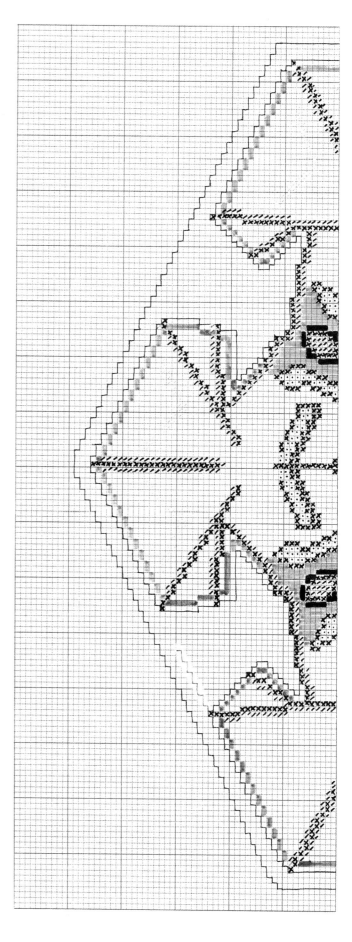

#30
BRIGHT PINK

WHITE
#1

71

See Color Plate 37   *page 57*

Yellow, gold and white snowflake

The colors are:

1 white

4 light yellow

5 medium yellow

7 dark yellow

14 orange

11 gold

109 grey

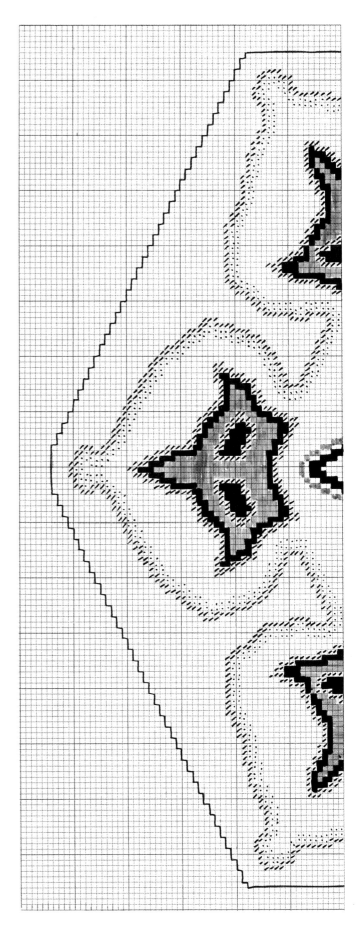

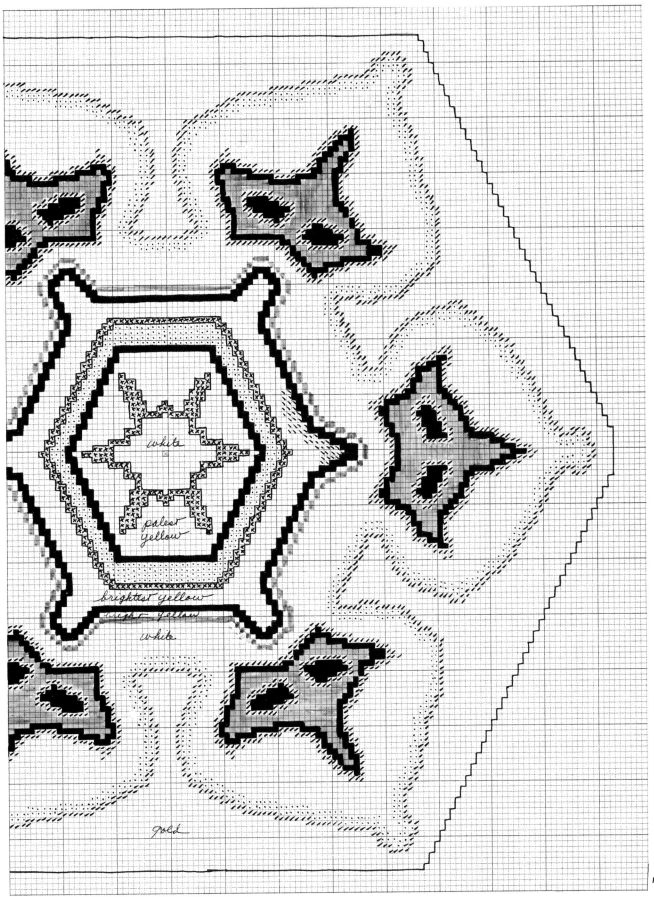

white

palest
yellow

brightest yellow

bright yellow

white

gold

73

Purple, black and brown snowflake

The colors are:

- □ 1 white
- ○ 45 light lavender
- ╱ 46 lavender
- · 42 purple pink
- ✗ 44 purple
-   93 gold-brown
- ■ 120 black

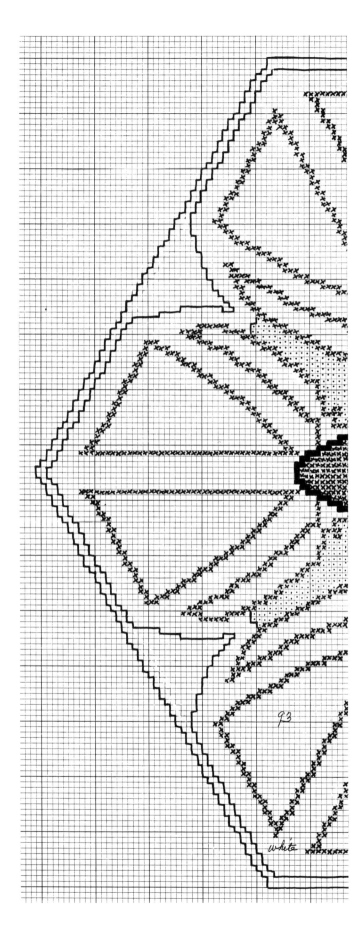

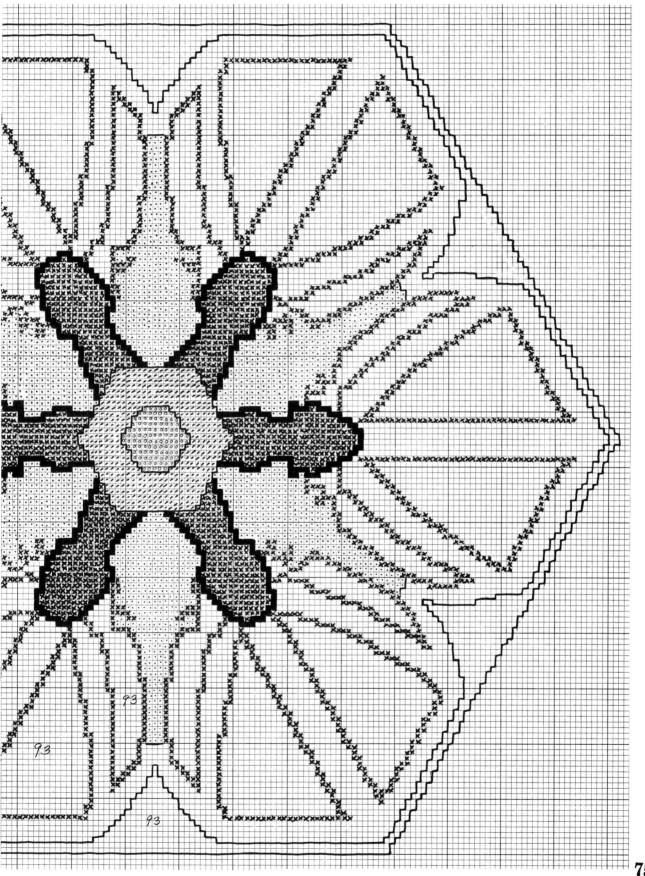

93

93

93

75

See Color Plate 39 *page 58*

Yellow, black and white snowflake

I couldn't resist putting some spider webs in the center of this design.

Spider Web directions

Following Chart B, working one spider web at a time, place them as indicated in Chart A. Put in the 8 stitches as directed in Chart B. Then finish the web as follows:

Bring the needle and yarn up to the left of the stitch at (2) Go over this stitch and then under it from right to left and go under the stitch at (3). Be sure to wrap the stitches only, and not the canvas with them. Now go back over and under this stich and under (4). Continue in this manner, wrapping around 2 stitches, building your web from the center to the outside until it is full, without crowding too much. Go through to the back of the canvas and end off.

The colors are:

- • 7 yellow

- ■ 120 black

- ▫ 1 white

- ⁄ 109 grey

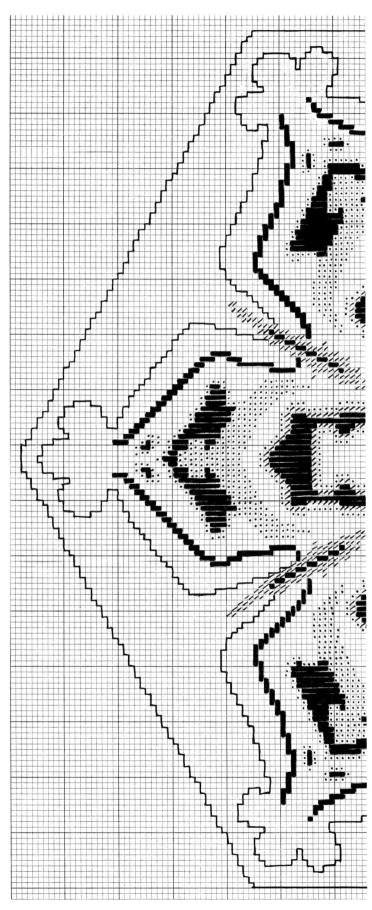

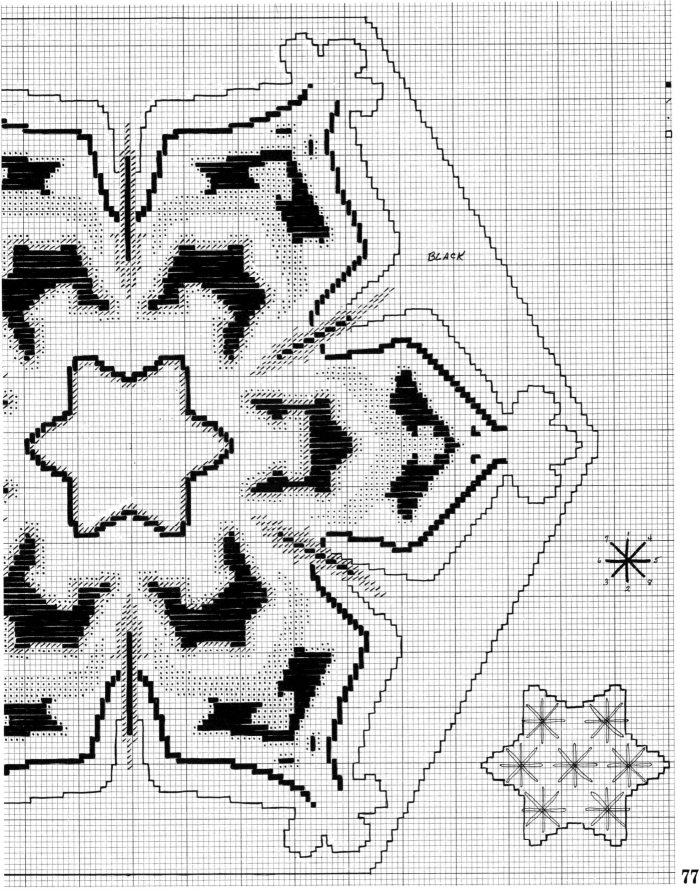

BLACK

See Color Plate 38   *page 58*

Paper weight

The colors are:

Center circles

    1 white

    30 light pink

    31 bright pink

Middle circles

    8 gold

    7 yellow

    5 yellow

Outer circles

  ▱ 77 green

  · 78 green

  ✕ 29 pink

  ───────

  ◼ 62 aqua

  ╱ 63 aqua

  ▱ 64 aqua

    1 white

  ▒ 102 grey

    3 cream background

78

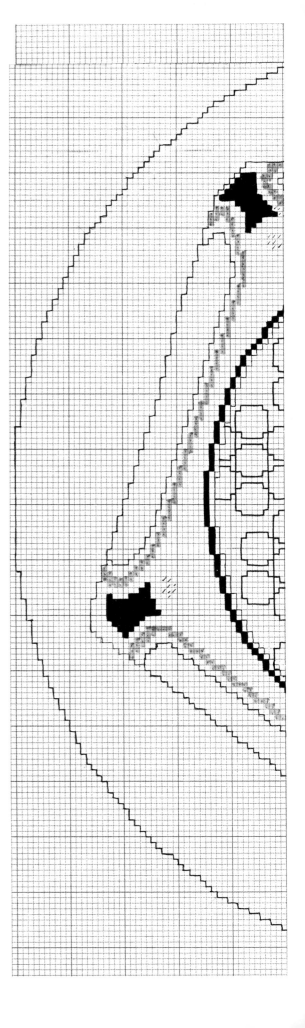

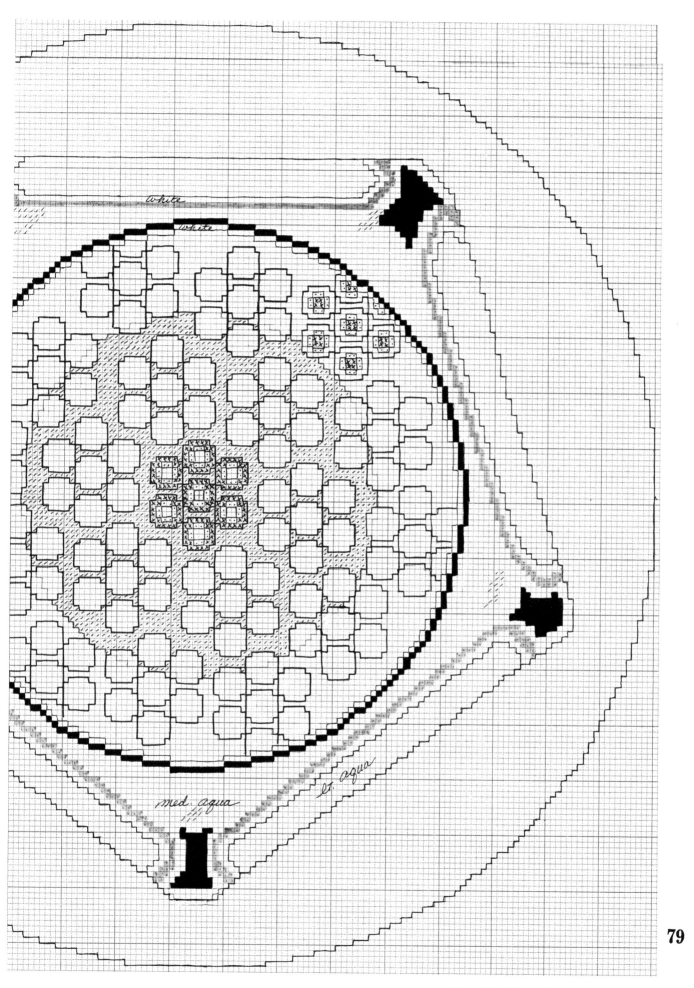

white

white

med. aqua

lt. aqua

See Color Plate 41 page 59

8 Adaptations of Plate 24 of Four Way Bargello

Turquoise and green regular bargello

I took the same 4-2 step design as the green and yellow pillow piece, but by shading it differently and breaking up the larger ground areas it really becomes a new pattern. This could go on indefinitely or a border of green would make a nice finish. My worked piece measures 12¾″ square. It was worked on #16 mono canvas which actually counts 15 to the inch.

On #14 canvas it should measure about 14½″
On #13 canvas it should measure about 15⅓″
On #12 canvas it should measure about 16¾″
On #10 canvas is should measure about 20″
All four strands of Nantucket Needleworks yarn was used in the following colors:

| 84 dark green

| 83 green

| 82 green

| 65 dark turquoise

| 64 turquoise

| 63 turquoise

| 62 turquoise

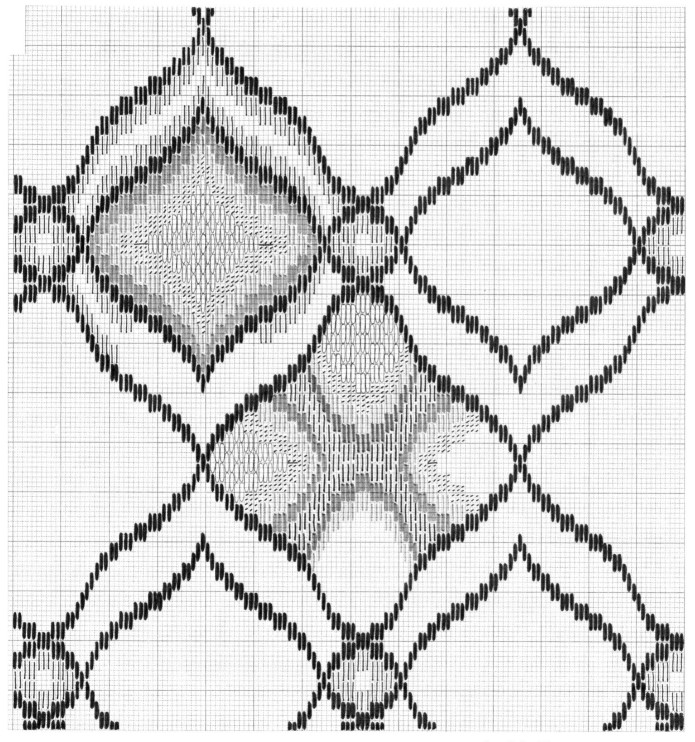

See Color Plate 42   *page 60*

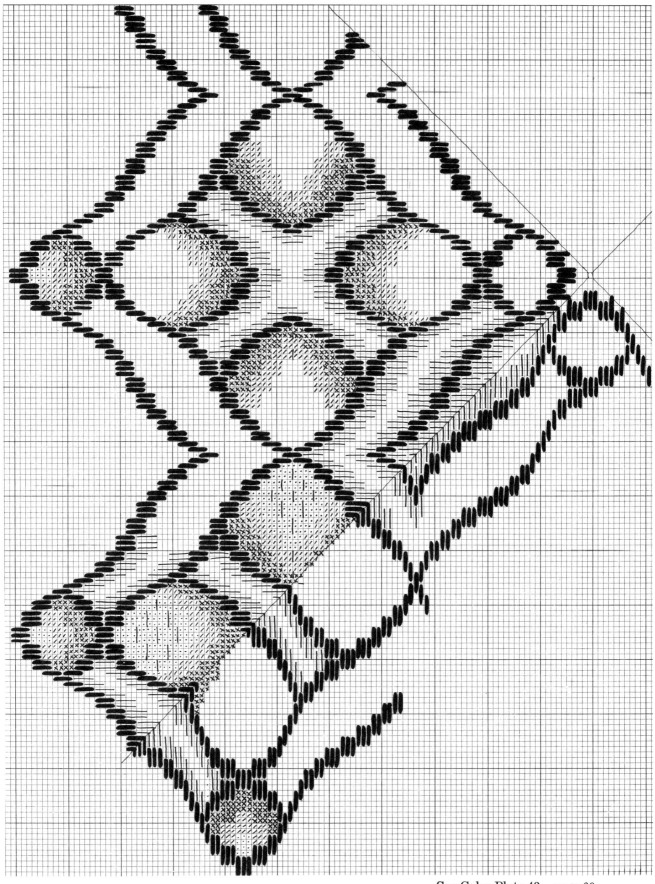

82

See Color Plate 43 *page 60*

Strawberry Patch four way bargello

I took the basic design and the same green of
No. 1 and made it into a four way bargello. This
was done on the same canvas and the design
measures 14¾″.

On #14 canvas it should measure 15¾″
On #13 canvas it should measure 17″
On #12 canvas it should measure 18⅓″
On #10 canvas it should measure 22″

A tent stitch background in another color would
finish this off nicely.
The pinks are:

  31 dark pink

  30 medium pink

  29 light pink

Copper and grey four way bargello

This is a 4-2 step using just a segment of the
original design. It would look quite different in
only one color range or using several color
families. The pattern could be made smaller by
working less rows or could go on indefinitely.
I worked on #16 mono canvas which really was
16 mesh to the inch, so the piece I did measures
15½″ square.

On #15 canvas it should measure 16⅓″
On #14 canvas it should measure 17½″
On #13 canvas it should measure 19″
On #12 canvas it should measure 20½″
On #10 canvas it should measure 24½″

All four strands of Nantucket Needleworks yarn
was used in the following colors:

21 dark copper

20 copper

19 copper

15 orange

Two strands of persian yarn in the
following colors:

311 dark grey blue

380 grey blue

381 grey blue

382 grey blue

84

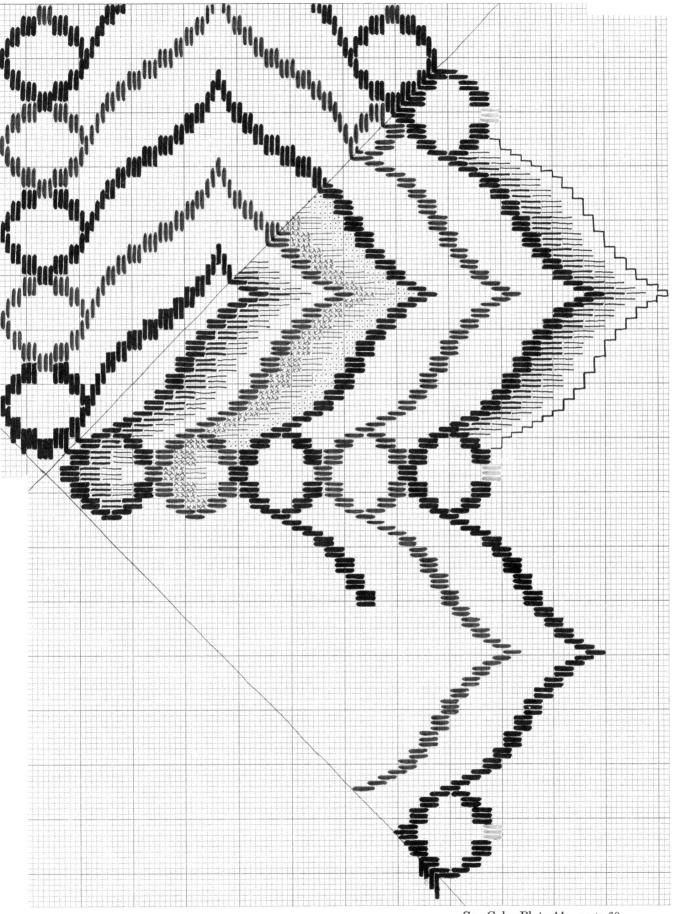

See Color Plate 44 *page 60*

9 An Assortment of Four Way Bargello Patterns

These are all done in a 4-2 step.

Red and white

I used a design from *Florentine Embroidery* by Barbara Snook (page 78) but did it in the four way manner. It was worked on #12 canvas with 3 strands of persian yarn. The design measures 16½".

On #16 canvas it should measure 12½"
On #15 canvas it should measure 13¼"
On #14 canvas it should measure 14"
On #13 canvas it should measure 15¼"
On #12 canvas it should measure 16½"
On #10 canvas it should measure 20"

The colors used were:

810 dark red

R10 red

R70 red

839 pink

860 pink

005 white background

See Color Plate 45   *page 61*

Blue, aqua, lavender center square and border

This started with the straight outline of the center square in color 733 blue. Then with 752 dark blue, I did a design that took me from one corner of the square to the other, on the outside of it. From the upper peak of this I moved up by one stitch and reversed the design and carried it out to the mitres. I decided that this was as large as I wanted it so did another straight border with the 733 blue. Then with the rest of the blues and other colors, I played in the areas created by these outlines.

The center square could have been worked in tent stitch with a monogram. It could also have been worked in a solid color either in regular or four way bargello.

This was worked on #14 canvas with 3 strands of persian yarn. The pattern measures 13¾″

On #16 canvas it should measure 12″
On #15 canvas it should measure 12-4/5″
On #13 canvas it should measure 14¾″
On #12 canvas it should measure 16″
On #10 canvas it should measure 19″

The colors used were:

- 733 blue for the borders
- 752 dark blue
- 754 blue
- 756 blue
- B43 blue
- 032 blue
- 773 dark aqua
- 783 aqua
- 793 aqua
- 765 aqua
- 621 dark lavender
- 631 lavender
- 641 lavender

88

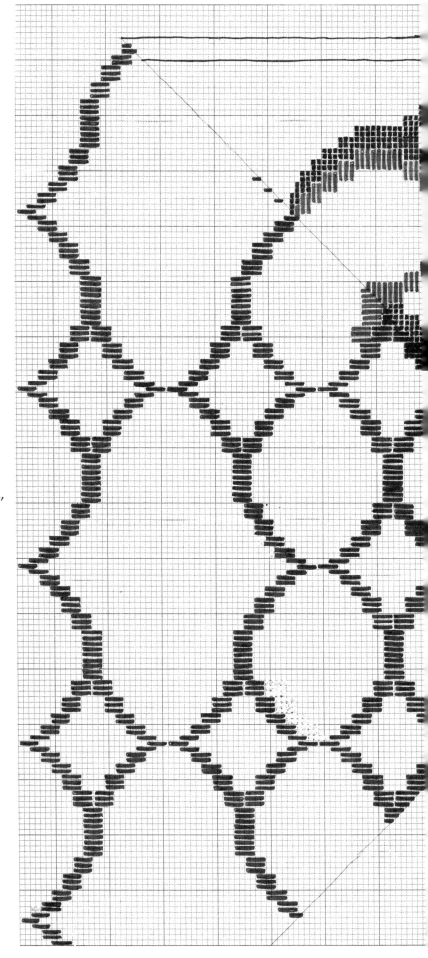

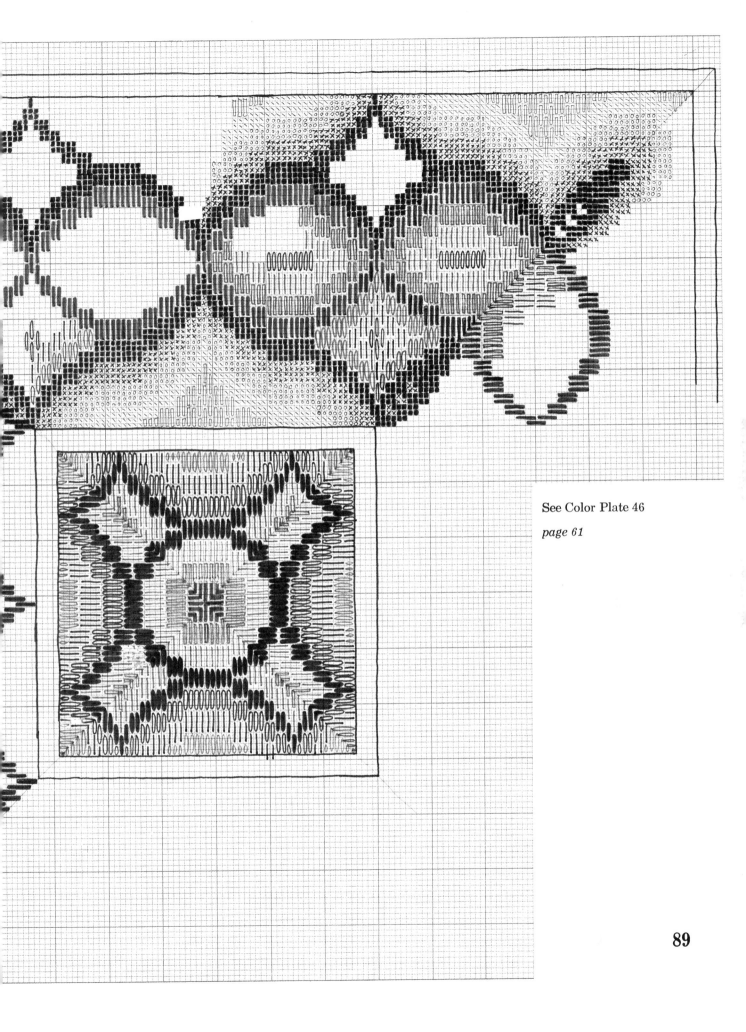

See Color Plate 46

page 61

Rose and blue with contour border

This would be a suitable design for one of these old cornerwise chairs since the design comes out that way on the canvas. To make this into a complete square "cornerwise" on the canvas, more canvas would be needed than there would be to finish when the canvas is square. This was worked on #12 canvas with 3 strands of persian yarn. The design measures 18¾" from one double peak to a double peak across the canvas. If measured from one long side of the border to the other it is about 16". This took about 6 ozs. of yarn.

If the peak to peak measurements are used they would be as follows:

#16 canvas should measure 14"
#15 canvas should measure 15⅓"
#14 canvas should measure 16½"
#13 canvas should measure 17¾"
#10 canvas should measure 23"

The colors used were:

236 dark rose

232 rose

282 rose

831 pink

837 light pink

323 dark blue

330 blue

385 blue

395 blue

396 blue

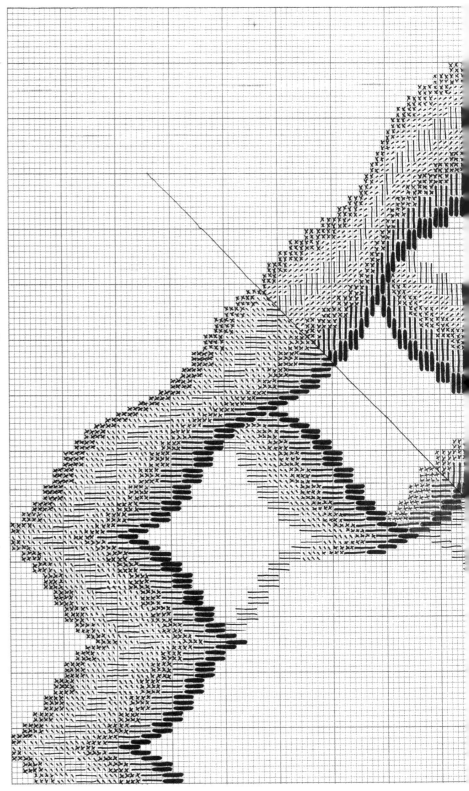

90

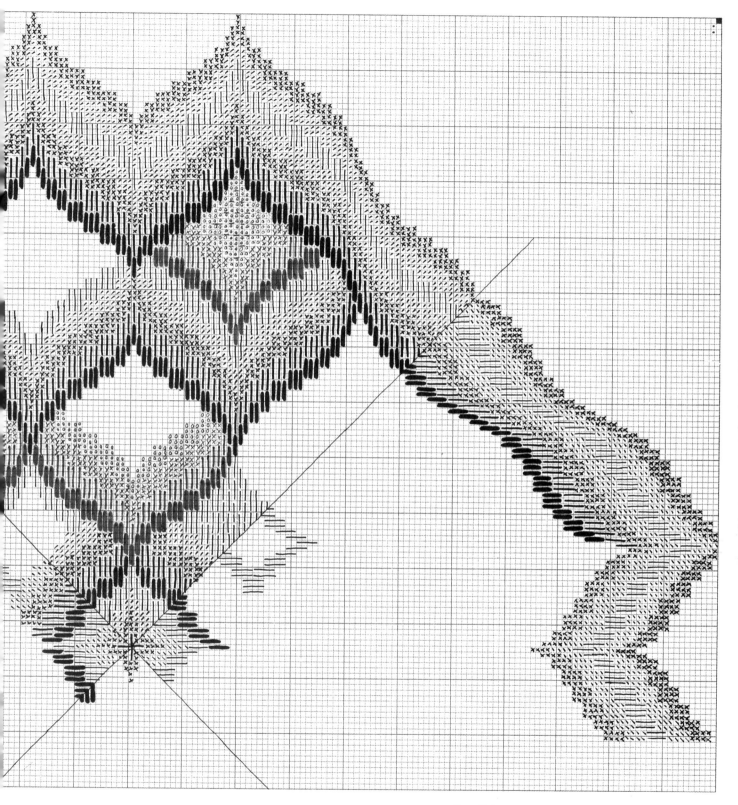

See Color Plate 47 *page 62*

Gold outline with pinks

This is a rather simple four way design using 4 strands of Nantucket Needleworks yarn on #16 canvas. The design measures about 12½″.

On #15 canvas it should measure 13⅓″
On #14 canvas it should measure 14½″
On #13 canvas it should measure 15⅓″
On #12 canvas it should measure 16¾″
On #10 canvas it should measure 20″

The colors used were:

9 gold outline

11 gold

25 dark red

26 pink

27 pink

28 pink

1 white

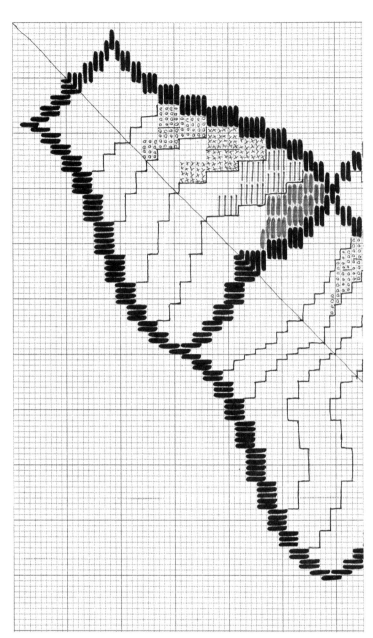

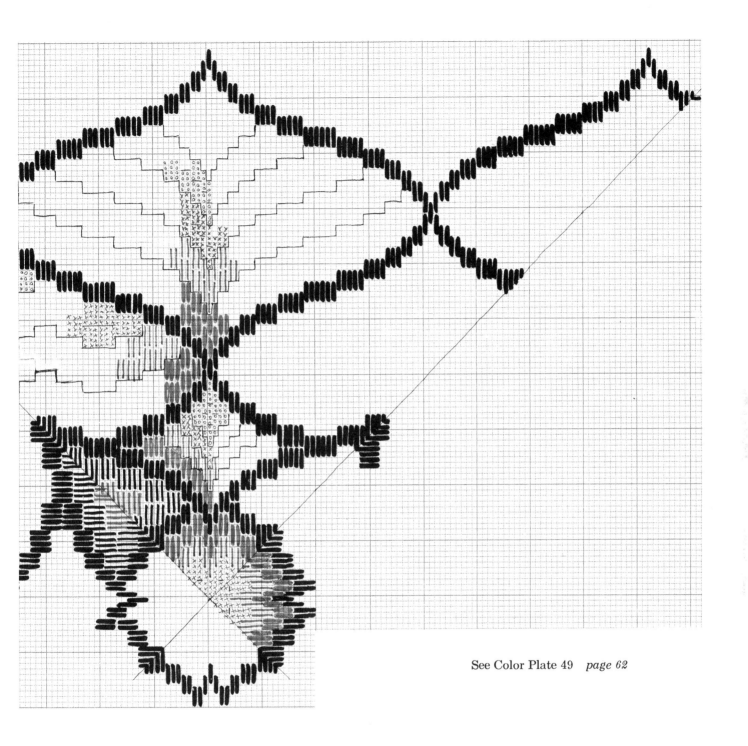

See Color Plate 49   *page 62*

Copper and grey

The black outline is identical to the gold outline in No. 4. The design becomes completely different by breaking up the areas in another way. The canvas and measurements are the same.
Two strands of persian yarn were used in the following colors:

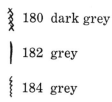

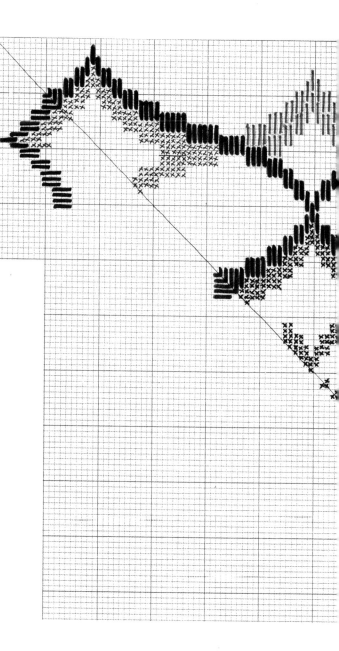

180 dark grey

182 grey

184 grey

Four strands of Nantucket Needleworks yarn were used in the following colors:

120 black

21 dark copper

20 copper

19 copper

15 orange

3 pale yellow

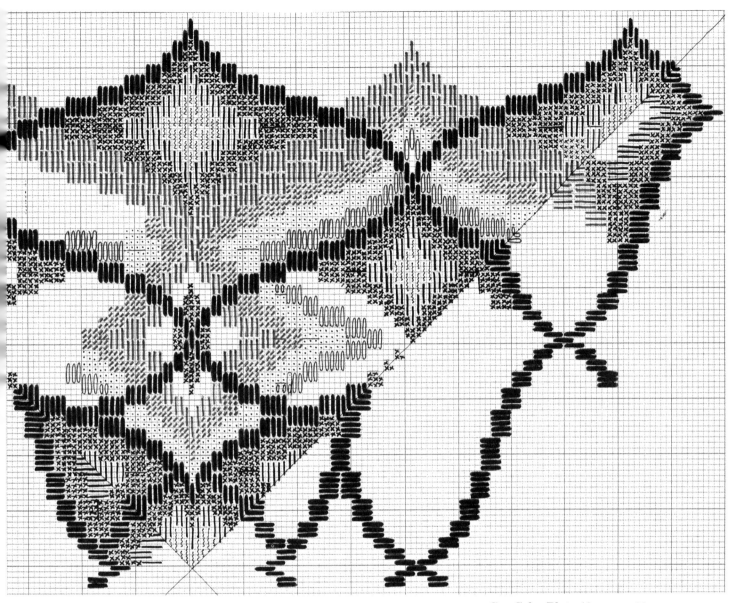

See Color Plate 48 *page 62*

Blue, aqua, green and orange hanging

This is a four way design worked off center to seem more like an abstract painting. It was worked on #12 canvas with 3 strands of persian yarn. It measures 15¾″ x 20″. On #10 canvas it would measure about 18″ x 24½″. It could be made considerably larger by extending the design. The colors used were:

742 dark blue

752 blue

754 blue

756 blue

763 aqua

728 aqua

738 aqua

748 aqua

504 green

G54 green

574 green

G74 green

960 orange

970 green

Y42 yellow

96

960
970
Y 42

97

See Color Plate 50 *page 63*

Spindrift—yellow, greens and orange

I did this for my niece, Cathy, as a pillow for a Christmas present. It was worked on #14 canvas with three strands of persian yarn. It measures 13¾″. This is a pattern which could easily be continued on, but if worked the same as the chart it should measure as follows:

#16 canvas should measure 12″
#15 canvas should measure 12¾″
#13 canvas should measure 14″
#12 canvas should measure 16″
#10 canvas should measure 19″

The chart indicates the dark olive green no. 540 lines only. The rest of the yellows and greens are in the following order:

040 pale yellow

458 light yellow

Y58 yellow

Y56 yellow

565 yellow green

446 mustard yellow

Y50 yellow

550 yellow green

545 yellow green

553 medium olive green

The center circle colors are:

 Y58 yellow

| 450 yellow

⋮ 444 orange

Y42 orange yellow

Y40 orange yellow

427 burnt orange

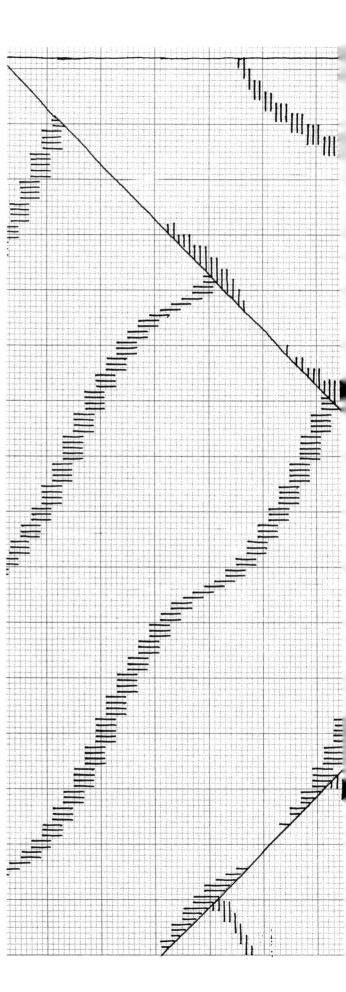

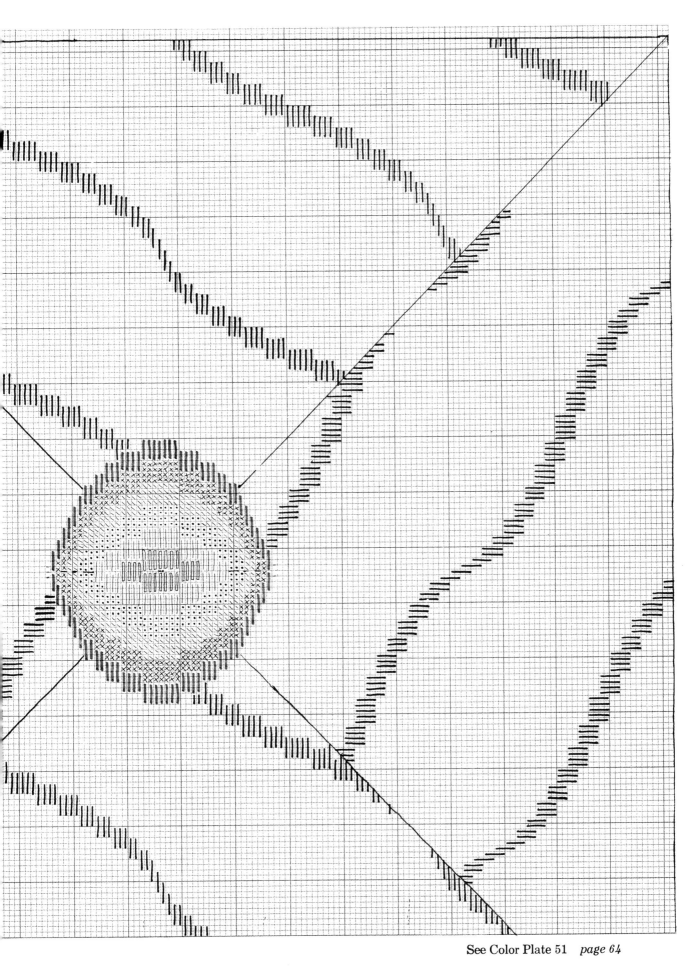

See Color Plate 51   *page 64*

Olive green oblong border

Mrs. Samuel Pierson designed and worked the original piece as shown in the color plates. She used 5 shades of olive green on a turquoise background. (I do not have a list of the exact colors or the size canvas it was worked on.)

I have made a chart, working from a small color transparency. There may be a stitch difference at the mitre, but it's a very close copy. She did the background in bargello, copying the established pattern, and finished with a border of 1 row of stitches all on the same step. This pattern would be an easy one to elongate still further by adding a few stitches to several of the steps on the long sides. It could also be made square by using just the short sides all around or the long sides, whichever part of the pattern you preferred.

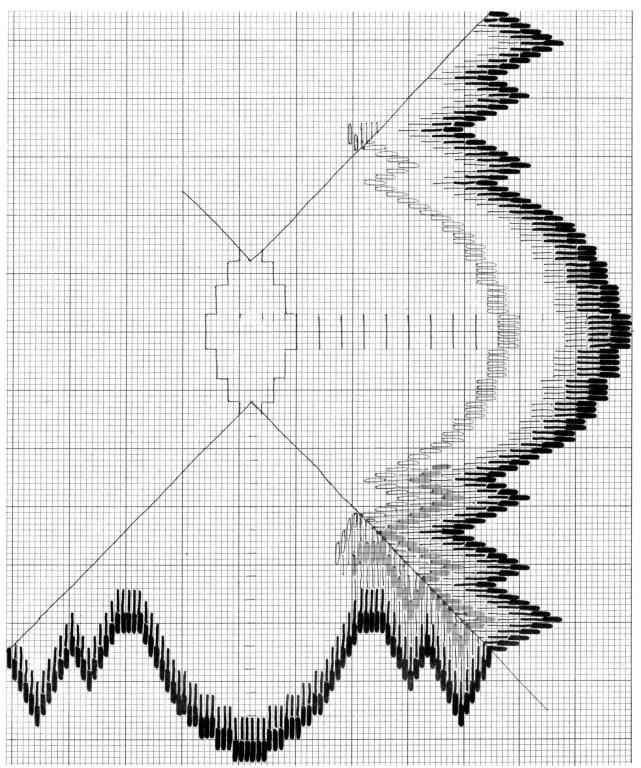

101

See Color Plate 52   *page 64*

10 Designs with Various Steps

Emerald and sapphire four way bargello

This is a 4-2 and a 6-2 step worked on #12 canvas with three strands of persian yarn. The design measures 14¾". However, with the background filled in and the edging stitch around, the completed piece measures 16⅓".

On #16 canvas it should measure 12¼"
On #15 canvas it should measure 13"
On #14 canvas it should measure 14"
On #13 canvas it should measure 15"
On #10 canvas it should measure 19½"

The colors used were:

G54 bright green

545 yellow green outline

510 dark green

G64 medium green

574 light green

G74 light green

340 dark blue green

750 dark turquoise

755 turquoise

760 turquoise

765 turquoise

781 turquoise

B43 pale blue

740 sapphire blue in the diamends

755 medium turquoise background

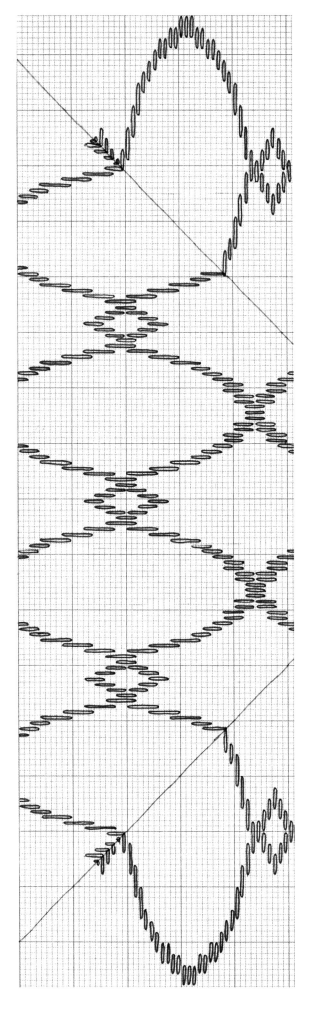

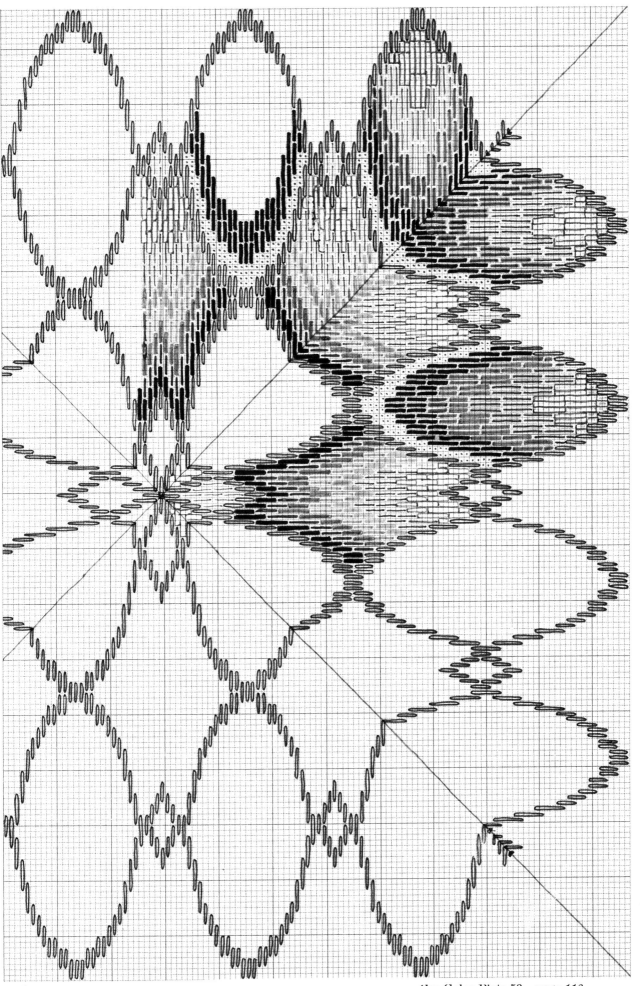

See Color Plate 53   *page 113*

Rose four way bargello

The steppings in this piece are 2-1, 3-1, 4-1, and 6-1 in various arrangements. Plate 54 shows it before it was finished. At this point a tent stich background in white or other color would look well. Also, the small parts of design in the outer corners could be eliminated to change the pattern. This would make a good regular bargello by repeating the center area of design across the canvas, instead of turning the corners.

The chart purposely shows varying stages of development so that you can see ways of using only part of the design, for example just the outer part as a border—the outer to middle section— the center section—or the center to middle section. I worked the background by following around row after row in the pattern as established.

This was on a #16 canvas, which again, measured close to 15 mesh to the inch, so my pattern measures 13½″

On #16 canvas it should measure 12¾″
On #14 canvas it should measure 14½″
On #13 canvas it should measure 15¾″
On #12 canvas it should measure 17″
On #10 canvas it should measure 20½″

Elsa Williams' tapestry yarn was used in the following colors:

N101 dark rose

N102 rose

N103 rose

N104 rose

N105 rose

N112 red

N114 light red

See Color Plate 54 & 55

page 114

105

Bright blue and olive green four way bargello

The steppings are varied as in No. 2

This is another border type design which could be used according to the suggestions as No. 2.

This was worked on the same canvas as No. 2 and measures 15″.

On #16 canvas it should measure 14″
On #14 canvas it should measure 16″
On #13 canvas it should measure 16¾″
On #12 canvas it should measure 18¾″
On #10 canvas it should measure 22½″

Elsa Williams' tapestry yarn was used in the following colors:

N521 dark blue

N522 blue

N523 blue

N524 blue

N525 blue

N402 dark green

N403A medium green

N404 light green

The color plate shows the center filled in following the established pattern using N524 blue. This design was inspired by a small sample of straight bargello that Sophia Hutchinson copied from an old piece she found. Mine is a little different.

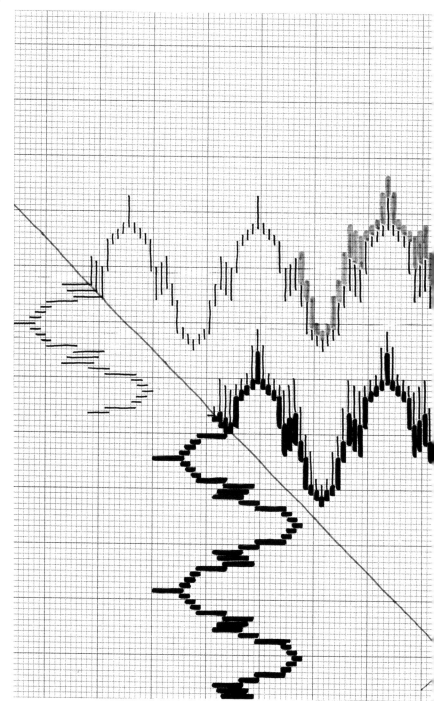

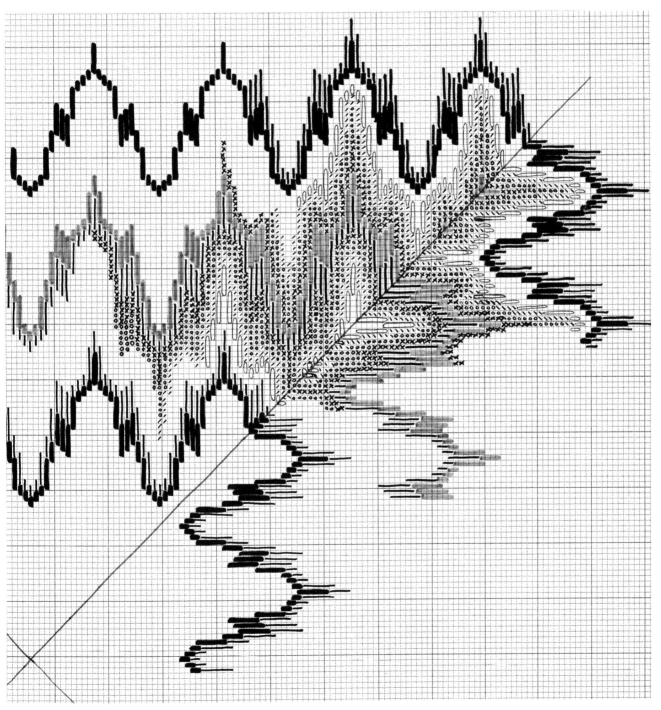

See Color Plate 56   *page 115*

Orange and gold-brown quarter design

This is a very large design. I started it as just
a regular bargello, but then had to see it as a four
way design. My canvas allowed me to do only a
little more than a quarter of it. When Sophia
Hutchinson saw this she couldn't resist calling
it my "plan ahead" design. The steppings are
like No. 2.

Plate 57 shows a wide border to be repeated
as a regular bargello both across and up and down
or just as a border. Plate 58 shows a narrower
part of the border carried around the corner. The
color plate shows where I reversed the inner
gold-brown four rows to form the center part.
I worked this on the same canvas as Nos. 2 and 3,
and if the design was fully completed it would
measure 22½". The complete design on #10
canvas with more subtle shading would make
a nice rug. I would suggest a couple of inches in
a solid color around the edges.

Elsa Williams' tapestry yarns were used in the
following colors:

N311 dark orange

N312 orange

N313 orange

N314 orange

N305 yellow

N712 dark brown

N301 gold-brown

N302 gold-brown

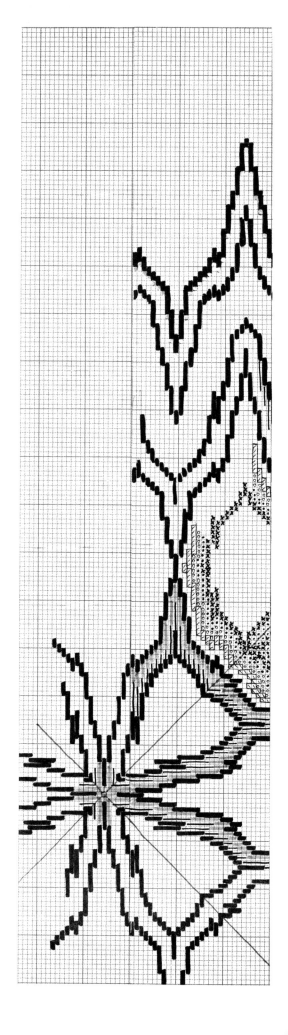

See Color Plate 59 *page 116*

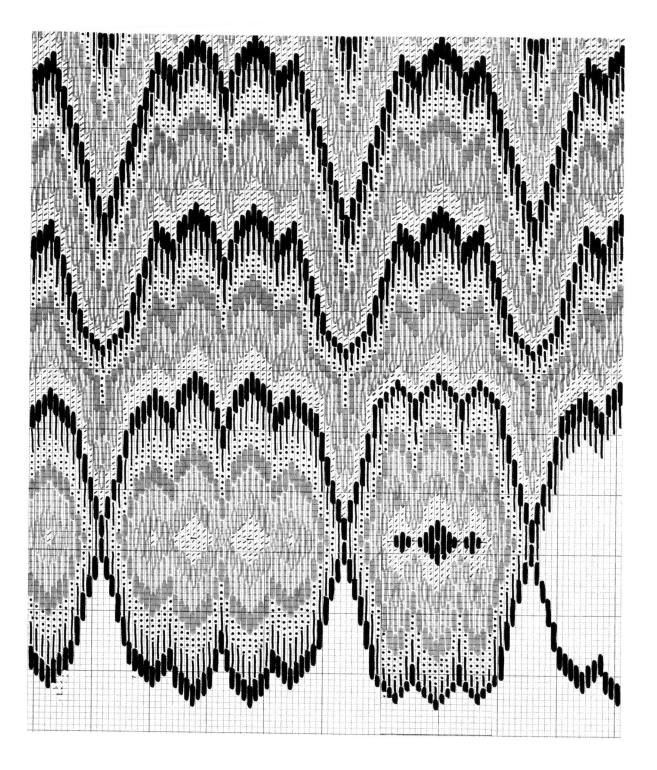

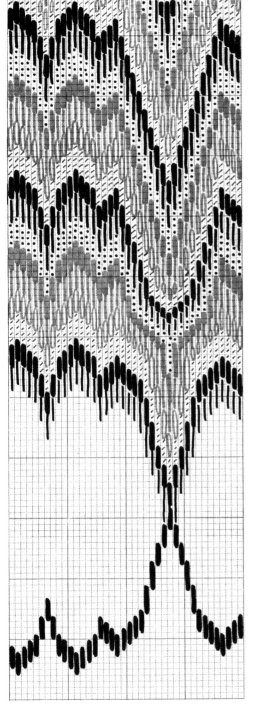

See Color Plate 60   *page 117*

Regular bargello in aqua and taupe

This is an assorted stepping of 2-1, 4-1, 5-1, and 6-1. It was worked with Elsa Williams' tapestry yarn on #13 lock weave canvas. The coloring in this is quite soft and could make a nice upholstery if worked on #16 canvas.

The colors used were:

N900 white

N805 off white

N714 taupe

N713 taupe

N416 pale green

N516 aqua

N515 aqua

11 Aztec Type Patterns

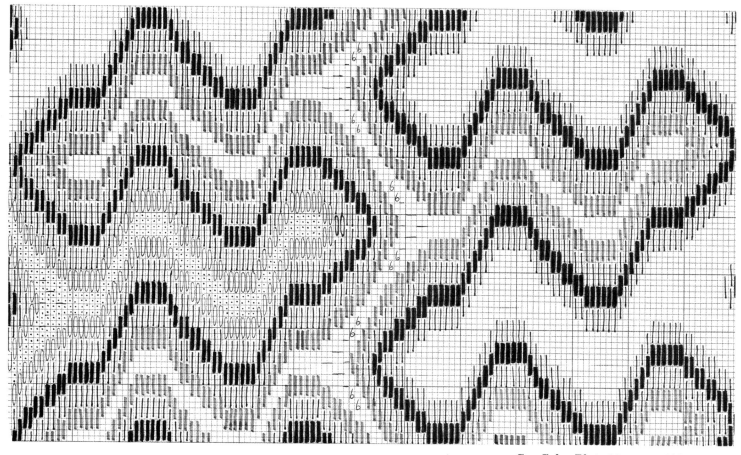

See Color Plate 61   *page 118*

Red, purple and orange

This was inspired by a room pictured in *House Beautiful* a couple of years ago. It would make a colorful pillow or a stunning wall hanging. My piece was worked on #14 canvas with 3 strands of persian yarn which would be suitable for a pillow or bench cover. For a hanging I would suggest #10 or #12 canvas. Three strands would still cover on #12 canvas, but four or five strands would be needed for #10. This is a 4-2 step.

The design isn't centered on the canvas and it doesn't seem to matter.

The colors used were:

R50 red

839 pink

633 purple

643 light purple

965 orange

Y40 yellow

Plate 53 Emerald and sapphire four way bargello *Chart, pages 102-103*

Plate 54

Rose four way bargello

Chart, page 105

Plate 55

Rose four way bargello

Chart, page 105

114

Plate 56   Bright blue and olive green four way bargello   *Chart, pages 106-107*

Plate 57

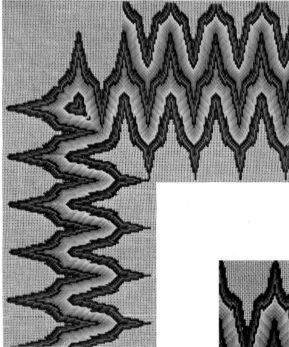

Plate 58

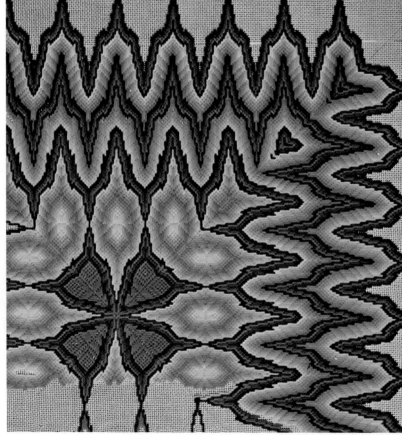

Plate 59

Orange and gold-brown quarter design

Chart, pages 108-109

116

Plate 60   Regular bargello in aqua and taupe   *Chart, pages 110-111*   **117**

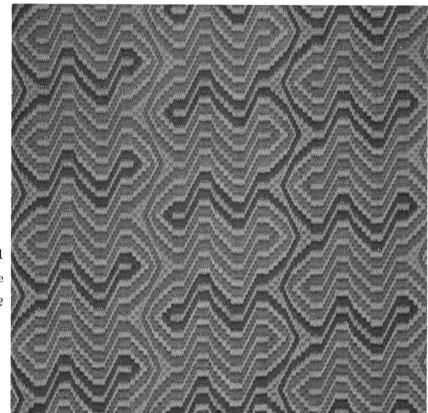

Plate 61

Red, purple and orange

Chart, page 112

Plate 62

Black, brown and white

Chart, page 121

118

Plate 63   Four Way Bargello Mini Patterns   *Chart, pages 122-123*

Plate 64   Tissue Box Covers and Wastebasket   *Chart, pages 125-131*

Plate 65   Four Foxes Tray   *Chart, pages 133-135*

Black, brown and white

This is a simplified version of the red, purple and orange pattern. While working the first pattern, I kept thinking of it in these colors. I also felt that the lines needed to be more angular and simpler for the starkness of the colors. This was worked on #14 canvas with three strands of persian yarn. This is a 4-2 step.

The colors used were:

| 050 black

| 201 brown

| 005 white

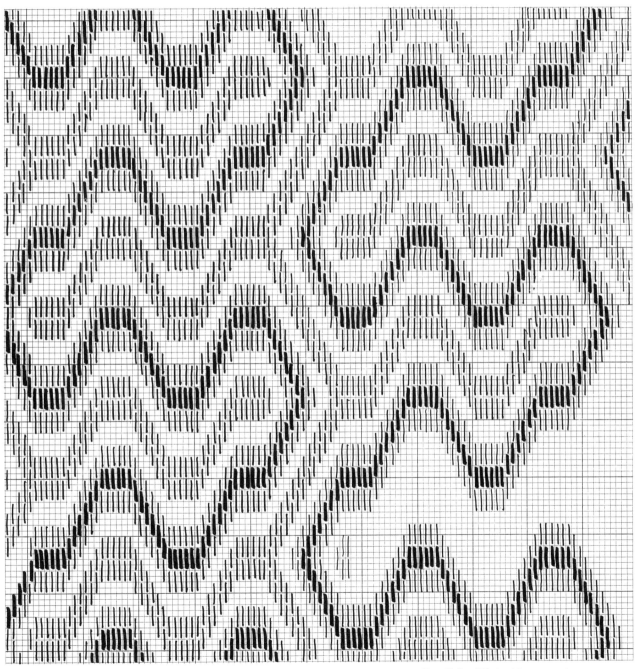

See Color Plate 62   *page 118*

Three Four Way Bargello Mini Patterns

These patterns make good coasters or pincushions. On #14 mono canvas they measure approximately 4½" square. They can also be used as a repeat pattern for larger pieces.

⅓ yard of Elsa Williams' tan 26" wide canvas will make 10 coasters. (2 strips of 5). All 3 of these designs use 60 threads of canvas. They are all a 4-2 step.

Measure off 5 squares across between selvedges. Start 3 threads in from selvedge and leave about 11 threads between squares. Count in 30 threads from each edge of square (center hole). With a pencil mark diagonal lines from each corner of the center hole to the corners of the square. These are the mitre lines so be sure that they are accurate.

Start with the dominant (completed) shade on the chart and work around with each color rather than working a quarter at a time. Use 3 strands of persian yarn.

NOTE: The plates show a number of variations in colors of these coasters and pincushions. Some of them were done by several women of St. Matthew's Church in South Norwalk for a Christmas fair, some were done by Mrs. Robert McKay of New Canaan, so I do not have a list of the colors used.

To finish coasters:

Block the needlepoint. Turn under about ½" of canvas. Blind stitch a piece of felt to the back. Cut the felt about ¼" larger than

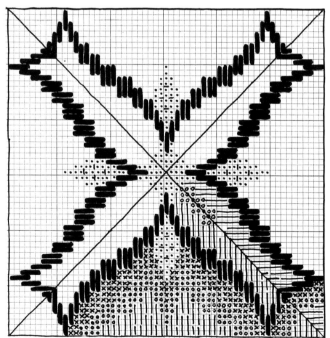

See Color Plate 63

page 119

See Color Plate 63

page 119

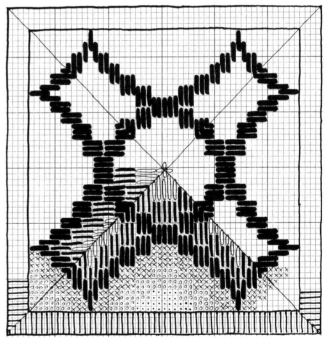

the actual size of the coaster and cut the corners so they will be mitred when turned under. This eliminates extra bulk at the corners.

To make a pincushion. Stitch a suitable piece of fabric to the needle-point—right sides facing each other—leaving 1 edge open. Trim edges leaving about ½" seam. Trim corners and turn right side out. Make a similar cover of muslin or any thin cotton fabric. Stuff this with kapok or other suitable suffing. Sew up the last edge of this inside "pillow", put it inside of the needlepoint cushion case and blind stitch the opening of this together.

123

Two Tissue Box Covers and a Wastebasket

Materials:

>1 straight sided oval metal wastebasket 11½" high x 25¾"
>   around
>1 O P Craft wooden tissue box cover
>Velverette glue
>small jar water base paint to match background
>yarn
># 220 or 280 sandpaper
>a piece of 16 mono canvas 16" x 21" for tissue box
>a piece of 16 mono canvas 15" x 29" for basket
>size 20 tapestry needles
>Nantucket Needleworks yarn—1 sk. of background for
>   tissue box, 2 sks. for basket
>1 sk. each of design colors for both

NOTE: persian yarn can be used by working with 2 strands for the bargellow and Elsa Williams' yarn can also be used for the bargello.

First prepare the canvas by turning under ¼" hem and machine or hand sew—or instead of turning a hem, tape with masking tape or baste bias binding on edges.

WASTEBASKET

Prepare the canvas as for the tissue box cover. Mark off the outline, then mark the middle of the long edge 22 rows from top line to top of stitch. This will be the center (low point) of the design. Start working the bargello from the middle to the left edge and then from the middle to the right edge. From here on work completely across from one edge to the other. The lightest shade of the bargello is also the background color so I worked 4 rows of tent stitch between each 4 rows of bargello for background. A couple of rows of tent stitch should be worked at the top and bottom of the piece for turning under for the finishing.

TO FINISH THE WASTEBASKET COVER

Block the needlepoint. Turn long edges under and machine stitch or use Stitch Witchery to secure. Stitch the 2 short ends together so that the piece fits snugly over the basket. Slip the cover over the basket. Use a little glue here and there at top to keep it from slipping down.

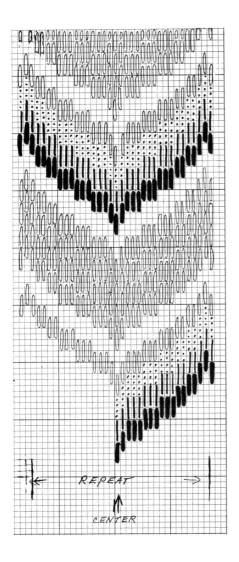

REPEAT

CENTER

TISSUE BOX COVER #1

Mark off your canvas according to the outline of the chart. My #16 canvas counted 15. If you get a piece that is a true 16, add to each end of pattern. Work the bargello pattern first. Notice that the pattern varies slightly. This was done to get the proper measurements. When your bargello pattern is completed, work the background in tent stitch using only 3 strands of the Nantucket yarn. The little tassels are put in last, using a full piece of yarn doubled. Make a rya knot at the bottom of each swag.

The colors used in the cover shown were light pink to red, 29, 30, 31, 32. Since the lightest pink of the design is the same color as the background, I had to work the background in tent stitch allow the design to be seen. If another color or shade was used, then bargello could have been worked throughout. A couple of rows of tent stitch should be worked at the bottom edges and around the top opening.

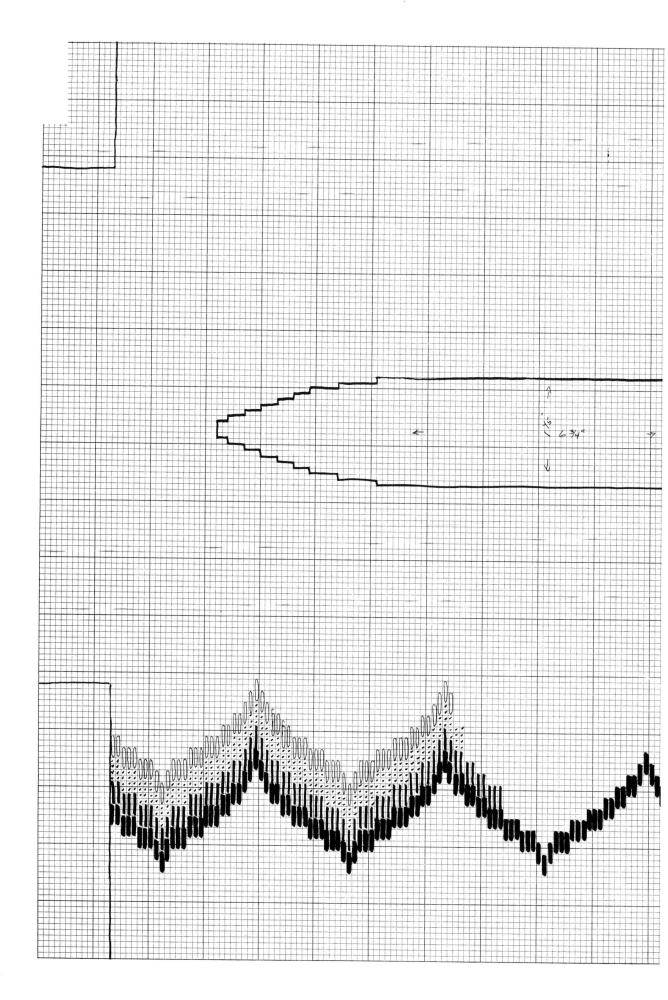

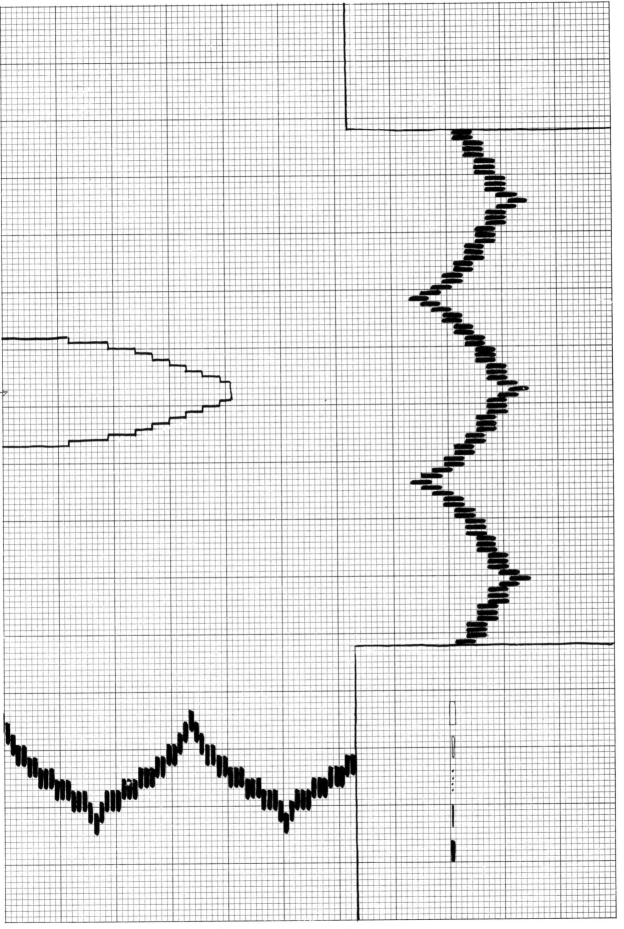

See Color Plate 64   *page 120*

TO FINISH THE TISSUE BOX COVER

First, sand the box inside and out to eliminate any roughness. Wipe clean. Then paint the inside, the bottom edges and the edge of the top opening. It should have at least 2 coats of paint. Block the needlepoint. Stitch the corners together and trim away the canvas, leaving about ¼″ at seams. Cut out the top opening leaving about ½″ of canvas for gluing under. Turn under about ½″ of canvas at bottom edges and glue to box.

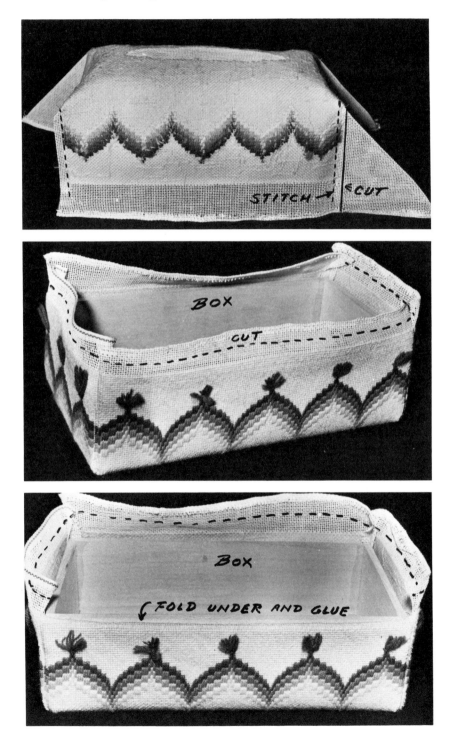

128

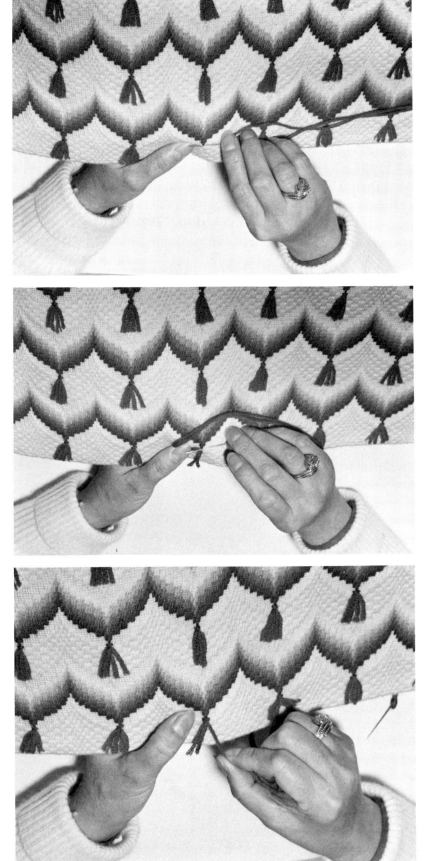

Insert needle from right to left under thread of canvas just below single stitch. Pull yarn through leaving about an inch for first half of tassel.

With yarn above, insert needle from right to left under the thread to the right of the previous thread of the canvas.

Pull yarn through and pull tight to form knot. Trim evenly to complete (Rya knot tassel)

TISSUE BOX COVER #2 BOUTIQUE

Materials

    1 DekCo tissue box cover # 02-204 or O.P. Crafts 1136
    1 small jar of paint to match bottom color
    #220 or 280 sandpaper
    Velverette glue
    a piece of #16 mono canvas 20″ x 20″
    1 skein each of Nantucket Needleworks yarn
    5 shades of one color, 4 shades of another color

Prepare the canvas as for tissue box #1. Outline the center hole of the canvas, draw the mitre lines as shown. Then work according to chart. Work tent stitch below the bargello around the bottom edges to fit box. Finish as for tissue box #1.

The colors used were:

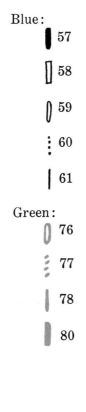

Blue:
    57
    58
    59
    60
    61

Green:
    76
    77
    78
    80

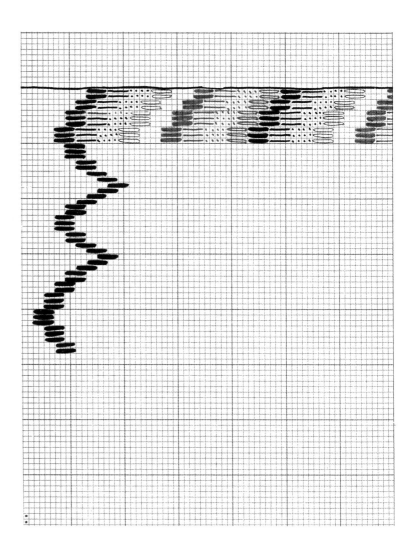

131

See Color Plate 64 *page 120*

The Four Foxes Tray

The fox idea came when I was showing the rose four way design, (chapter 10, design 2), to Joan Keever. Immediately she could see fox heads with those big ears in the corners. So she suggested that I chart a fox's head and let her work it. The bargello worked out fine for the ears, top of the head, and the sides of the cheeks. The rest of the face we did in tent stitch. We had just put the Sudbury trays in our store, and since we wanted to do a needlepoint for one anyway, we decided to use the fox's head in the four corners of one. Rather than having them all alike, I decided to have the eyes different in each. Then we added the hunting horn in the center.

The tent stitch is worked in one direction for 2 of the heads and in the opposite direction for the other 2. The rest of the tent stitch is worked as usual.

No. 18 mono canvas was used with 2 strands of Nantucket yarn and for a couple of colors 1 strand of persian.

The tray measures 15½″ x 23½″ with an opening of 10¼″ x 18″. A piece of canvas 17″ x 25″ should be used and a finished work area should be 11¼″ x 19″ so as to be sure the needlepoint is tucked well under the wood. When the piece is finished and blocked, it can be cut to fit the entire tray, rather than just a little larger than the opening. It will stay in position better. A small dab of glue at the corners will keep it in place.

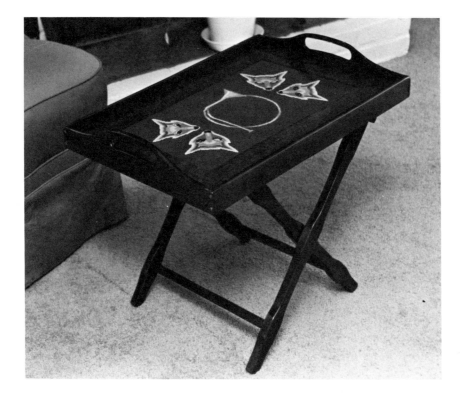

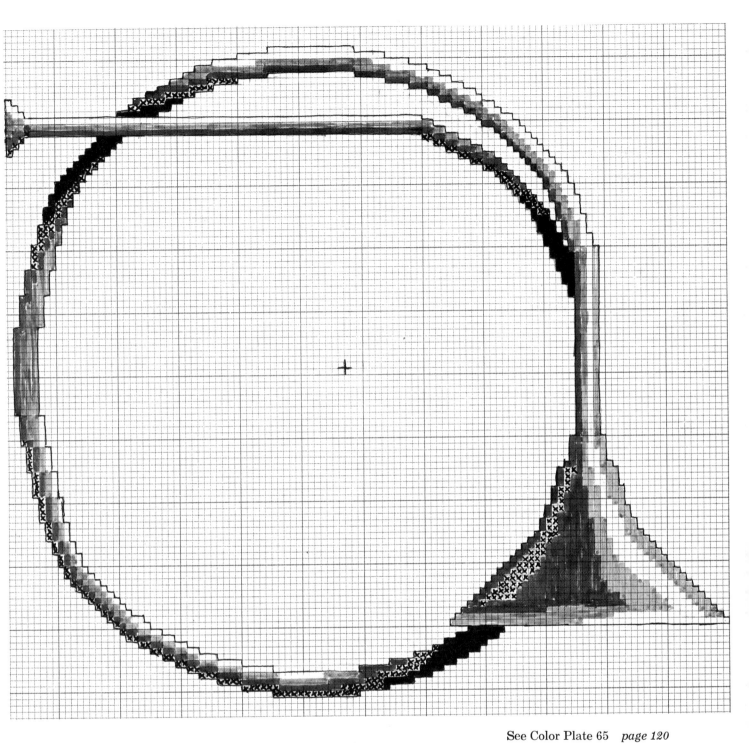

See Color Plate 65 *page 120*

Horn   Background

■ 11 dark gold

              79 green

✕ 10 gold

▩   8 gold

442 gold (persian)

□   3 light yellow

133

The colors used were:

Foxes

Bargello

❚	217	dark copper (pers.)
❙	20	copper (Nant.)
X	21	copper
❪	19	copper
❘	15	orange
❚	94	cream
❪	3	page yellow

Tent Stitch

■	120	black
▪	21	copper
·	20	copper
^	19	copper
+	15	orange
✓	94	cream
·	3	pale yellow
□	1	white (in eyes)
▨	111	grey

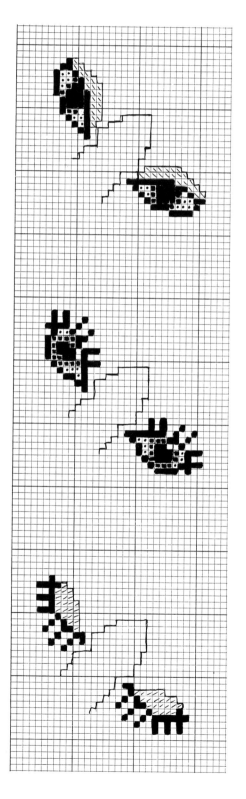

NOTE: The blank areas in the forehead and snout are to be filled in with the color suggested surrounding the areas. I left them that way for easier counting.

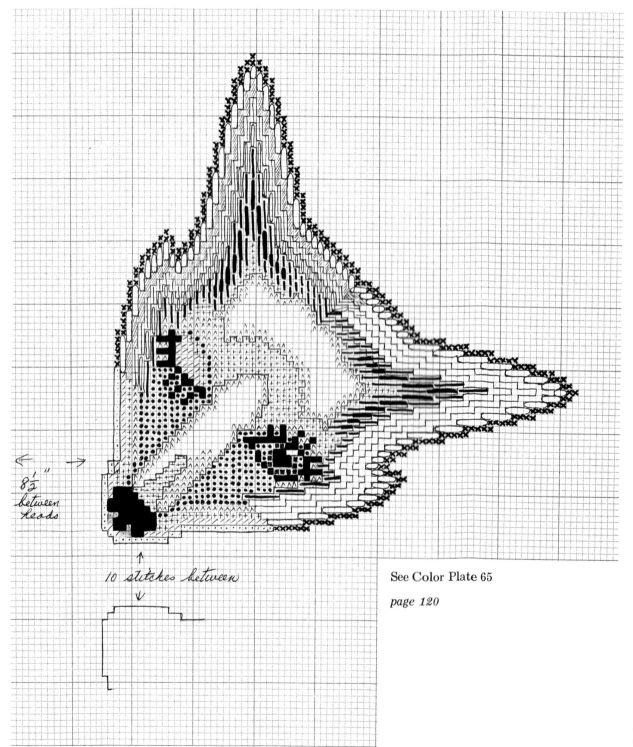

8½" between heads

10 stitches between

See Color Plate 65

page 120

Bibliography

Color Treasury of Rugs and Tapestries
Crescent Books

Florentine Embroidery, Barbara Snook
Charles Scribner's Sons, N.Y. 1967

Snowflakes, W. A. Bentley and W. J. Humphreys
Dover Publications, N.Y.